ANTI-HERO

THE SPY WHO MASTERMINDED THE LARGEST ESPIONAGE RING IN USA HISTORY

ETHAN QUINN

© Copyright Ethan Quinn 2018. All rights reserved.

No part of this book may be reproduced in any form without permission in writing from the author. Reviewers may quote brief passages in reviews.

Polite Note for the Reader's Attention

Anti-Hero has been written in UK English and certain words or phrases might vary from US English. This is except when loyalty to other languages and accents are deemed appropriate.

ISBN-13: 978-1726364812
ISBN-10: 172636481X

For Heidi and Nora

CONTENTS

Fritz Joubert Duquesne: Anti-Hero 7
Chapter 1: The Early Years 16
Chapter 2: The Man Who Hid The Kruger Millions 23
Chapter 3: Captive of Sin 30
Chapter 4: A Lifelong Hatred 37
Chapter 5: Cape Town Betrayal 46
Chapter 6: Professional Manipulator 53
Chapter 7: A Bid For Freedom 60
Chapter 8: Independence 71
Chapter 9: A Different Life 78
Chapter 10: War, At Last 87
Chapter 11: A Necessary Death 94
Chapter 12: The Fall of Lord Kitchener 101
Chapter 13: Desperation 108
Chapter 14: The Mask of Insanity 115
Chapter 15: The Last Escape 124
Chapter 16: Hiding In Plain Sight 128
Chapter 17: A Hatred Renewed 134
Chapter 18: A Hero's End 137
Chapter 19: The Greatest Roundup In US History 144
Chapter 20: Legacy 151
About Ethan Quinn 153

Fritz Joubert Duquesne: Anti-Hero

It is often said that truth is stranger than fiction.

For every fictional creation—a character, a scenario, a plot—there exists a real-life seed from which such imagined circumstances were born. It is believed that the world's most beloved fictional spy, James Bond, is based on author Ian Fleming's real-life espionage experiences. Baker Street's most renowned detective, Sherlock Holmes, was inspired by a Scottish surgeon named Joseph Bell, who possessed Holmes' deduction skills, albeit to a much smaller degree.

However, when it comes to little-known war hero Fritz Joubert Duquesne, it is likely that no fictional adaptation could come close to dramatising his life to the standards which would be necessary to do it justice. Even in the realm of fiction, the story of Fritz Duquesne may seem too far-fetched for any kind of mythical portrayal.

While Fritz Duquesne lived a life with more dramatic events than a Hollywood action movie, he is most famously remembered for one particular aspect of his colourful history: masterminding the biggest spy ring in USA history during the time of the Second World War.

To eventually achieve such bittersweet acclaim, Fritz Duquesne endured more hardships and manipulated more situations than most people could in a hundred lifetimes. His story is one brought about by an unquenchable desire for vengeance, stemming from a tragic incident involving the horrific slaughter of his family by a legion he himself was part of. This perceived betrayal then propelled Fritz Duquesne to establish himself as something of a mole inside the British government, using his military position to sabotage plans and wreak havoc on those he deemed responsible for the loss of his loved ones.

Duquesne's operations didn't always end with his intended result, and he regularly found himself at the mercy of those who wished for his head on a platter. However, with Harry Houdini-like skill, Fritz Duquesne somehow managed to evade death or capture for most of his life, allowing him to pursue treachery, sabotage, and vengeance. On the surface, it may appear as though Fritz Joubert Duquesne was both protagonist and antagonist of his own story. However, like so many of history's most infamous anti-heroes, Duquesne possessed a unique likability, regardless of his ultimate intentions. Indeed, Duquesne can be considered an outlaw, a rogue, and even a villain in some respects, but his actions were fuelled by the most basic of human experiences: heartbreak, vengeance, and in a sense, redemption.

To understand Fritz Duquesne's motivations for orchestrating the infamous spy ring for which he became known, it is important to look at the circumstances which led up to the event.

Fritz Duquesne, a South African Boer, was born in 1877 in East London, part of the British controlled Cape Colony. His family soon moved to the Nylstroom area of the South African Republic, where they started a farm. Right from an early age, Duquesne was thrown head first into a life of chaos, conflict, and death. The circumstances in which Duquesne regularly found himself forced him to become the die-hard soldier he was eventually known as. Before he had even reached his teenage years, Duquesne had already taken the life of a disgruntled gentleman who threatened his mother over a transactional dispute. Without hesitation, Duquesne picked up the man's own weapon and plunged it deep into his stomach, leaving him for dead. At the same age, Duquesne also opened fire on an invading tribe who attacked his family's settlement. These two incidents would set the tone for Duquesne's future life of unpredictable mayhem.

He spent much of his childhood between London and his home country of South Africa, where he completed university studies and eventually enrolled in British military service at the age of seventeen. During his first stint of military service, Duquesne spent considerable time away from his family, with whom he was unable to maintain contact. During a military siege in South Africa, Duquesne made his way back to his family's farm in Nylstroom, Modimolle. Upon his arrival, Duquesne was greeted with the heart-breaking sight that would forever change his life.

Duquesne discovered that his family's settlement had been reduced to ashes as a result of a scorched earth policy put in place by British officials. His family's house, their farm, and the entire surrounding area had been set alight on the instructions of British leader Lord Kitchener as part of the ongoing Anglo-Boer war. He was then informed that a gang of British soldiers had forcefully taken Duquesne's younger sister, Elbert, out into a desolate clearing and sexually assaulted her one by one. When her ordeal was over, she was then executed by the same soldiers with a point-blank shot to her head. Duquesne was then told that his uncle had also been publicly executed while other British soldiers and terrified citizens looked on.

Duquesne was then informed that his mother had endured trauma similar to his sister's, having been brutally sodomised by British soldiers. However, Duquesne's mother wasn't executed like her more unfortunate relatives. Instead, she had been taken to a British concentration camp where her torturous ordeals would continue. The fact that Duquesne's mother's torment hadn't yet ended filled him with an unspeakable rage that would drive his actions for the remainder of his life.

Duquesne, grief-stricken at the unnecessary cruelty shown his beloved family, made it his life's goal to avenge the deaths of those he loved. It was at this moment that he vowed vengeance against the British forces and, in particular, Lord Kitchener. In his mind, Duquesne held Lord Kitchener personally responsible for the destruction that had befallen his land, his family, and his heritage.

His first personal mission was to uncover the whereabouts of his mother, who he understood to be suffering in a British concentration camp. Duquesne infiltrated the camp, located east of Johannesburg, and there found his mother barely alive. Since she had been taken by British forces, she had been starved and left for dead. When Duquesne found her, in addition to her already excessive suffering, she had also contracted syphilis, either caused by her proximity to infected prisoners or possibly by being directly sexually assaulted by someone with the disease.

History books make no mention of exactly what Duquesne said to his mother during his final interaction with her. Given that she was currently at death's door, it's very likely that Duquesne knew he would never see her again once he exited the camp. On his way out, Duquesne was confronted by two camp guards who questioned his true reasons for being there. Duquesne shot and killed them both, then left for Cape Town. He never saw his mother again.

This would be the beginning of Duquesne's reign of terror against the British from within. During his time in Cape Town, South Africa, in 1901, Duquesne recruited twenty others in his efforts to bring down the British military, all of whom he believed harboured similar tendencies to his own. They had planned to set off explosives across all manner of British establishments: power plants, ammunition depots, railways, and so forth. However, one of the men whom Duquesne recruited betrayed them and revealed their intentions to other British officers. The whole group was arrested and sentenced to death.

Like many fictional heroes after him, Fritz Duquesne managed to escape death at the last moment. He then fled to the USA and underwent a significant transformation. It was here that Fritz Duquesne went into a life of journalism—worlds apart from the worn-torn battlefields and enemy manipulation he had become so accustomed to.

For the next decade or so, Duquesne remained in the USA working as a reporter. He soon manoeuvred his way into the life of President Theodore Roosevelt by becoming his personal shooting instructor.

However, Duquesne's hatred of the British still burned brightly. In 1914, he was recruited by the German army as a World War I spy. Assuming a fake identity, Duquesne set out for Brazil, where he remained for several years, allegedly using explosives to sabotage and sink over twenty British vessels, one on which Lord Kitchener was a passenger.

Following some risky insurance claims, Duquesne was arrested in the USA and faced either life imprisonment or execution. Not one to be restricted by the letter of the law, however, Duquesne pulled off an elaborate scheme which, even by today's standards, would appear to be beyond the realm of possibility.

Following his escape, Fritz Duquesne again made himself invisible for several years, assuming yet another fake identity. He settled into the life of a journalist for over a decade, but in his heart, he still possessed a deep yearning to destroy the British in any way possible. It was in 1936 that he accepted the role of intelligence officer for the German army, a position that began his orchestration of the largest spy ring in the USA at the time. Although Duquesne wasn't directly involved in sabotaging British forces, sabotaging their overseas allies was enough to keep him satisfied.

What later became known as the "Duquesne Spy Ring" was a total of thirty-three spies, strategically stationed across the USA, who used their espionage skills to obtain information that could be used to sabotage their enemy's war plans. These members opened restaurant establishments and shops and took service industry jobs to occupy positions that would convince their victims they were trustworthy.

For over five years, the Duquesne Spy Ring relayed their findings back to their German leaders, providing them with invaluable information that could then be used to bring down the Allied forces. It wouldn't be until 1941, following a two-year investigation into the suspected spy ring, that the FBI were finally able to intervene and ultimately take it down. Thanks to a handful of double agents within the FBI, eventually all thirty-three members of the ring were placed on trial, resulting in a collective three-hundred-year sentence.

Unfortunately, this would be one situation that the elusive Fritz Duquesne, also known at this point by several other names, couldn't manipulate his way out of. Finally, Fritz Joubert Duquesne's life of sabotage had ended. At his trial, Duquesne made his motivations clear to the world: he acted out of a desire for revenge against the British for their crimes against his country and his family. He was sentenced to eighteen years in prison, of which he served 13 years before being released due to ill health.

FBI director J. Edgar Hoover called this resounding defeat of the Duquesne Spy Ring the greatest spy roundup in U.S. history. It was later declared by the German forces that the collapse of the Duquesne Spy Ring was the final nail in the coffin for their espionage operations in the United States. It was around this time, perhaps not coincidentally, that the Allies began to gain significant control over their Axis enemies during World War II.

This introduction is meant to give you a brief overview of the circumstances that Fritz Duquesne endured, escaped, and endured again. To this day, Fritz Joubert Duquesne remains one of the most elusive yet celebrated figures in espionage history. Over the years, a handful of biographers have cast doubt over the accuracy of the stories about him, but the lack of information about this enigmatic anti-hero only adds more intrigue to his colourful life. The narrative that follows in this book aims to delve into the fine details of Fritz Joubert Duquesne's life based on accounts from biographers and newspaper sources as well as statements made by those involved in Duquesne's life and, of course, Duquesne himself. Since his legacy has come to light, Fritz Duquesne has been labelled with many terms: hero, villain, storyteller, raconteur, fraud, charlatan, saboteur, traitor, and many more, but however you might perceive him, there's no denying that Fritz Joubert Duquesne is one of the most fascinating figures in living history.

Chapter 1: The Early Years

Born to parents Abraham and Minna Duquenne on 21st December, 1877, it was only a matter of minutes before Frederick L'Huguenot Joubert Duquenne—later known as Fritz Joubert Duquesne—was thrust into a life or death scenario. In a run-down, backstreet house on the outskirts of East London, Fritz's first moments on this earth were of confusion, terror, and uncertainty.

The Duquenne family brought their son into the world to a soundtrack of violence taking place on the nearby war-ravaged Buffalo River. Sounds of gunshots and the clanging of steel on steel echoed in the distance as Abraham and Minna attempted to appease the cries of their newborn infant. For the first twenty-five years of his life, Fritz went by his family name of Duquenne. As the family was of French Huguenot heritage, the name was rooted in the French Du Quesne, which later evolved to Duquenne. It is unclear why exactly he adopted the variation we have become familiar with, but it was perhaps to distance himself from his Boer history. Throughout his life, Fritz Duquesne took on many disguises, many personas, all in the name of deceitful espionage. It seems that the name Duquesne was simply a way to honour his heritage and still remain a different person, all without straying too far from the ethnic roots he cherished so dearly.

Despite their living conditions, the Duquenne family were not poor by any means. They had settled into a port town near the Buffalo River due to its proximity to their fellow Huguenots. It was a convenient place to live, and perhaps one of the safest for their kind in the whole of East London.

Fritz's father, Abraham Duquenne, made his living through the hunting and trading of animal skins. Prior to his life in East London, he had traversed the South African hinterlands, killing and skinning all manner of ferocious wildlife and then flaying their skins or removing their tusks and horns. Abraham continued this trade during his East London years, gradually building up his fortune to provide a better life for his family. The family remained in East London for a few more years before returning to Nylstroom, South Africa. There, the Duequenne family purchased an isolated farm, two miles away from any kind of civilization. Abraham assumed it would be a place of peace and tranquillity for his family to escape the hazards of war. However, his assumptions were quickly turned on their heads.

It was on this farm where the young Fritz learned how to survive using only primitive skills. His father and uncle taught him to hunt for meat, milk cows, slaughter livestock, and defend himself with the use of Zulu weaponry. This last skill turned out to be vital for young Fritz, as he was forced to put his newfound self-defence skills into action at an age when most youngsters were still enjoying their carefree childish lifestyles.

In the spring of 1889, when Fritz was not yet a teenager, a Zulu warrior approached the Duquenne farm with the intention of trading a sack of vegetables for other goods. Fritz's mother, Minna, offered the Zulu a fair trade of alcohol, cloth, and an assortment of food in exchange for his vegetables. However, the Zulu quickly became irate with the offer, seeing it as an insult. It was unclear exactly why the Zulu didn't take kindly to this transaction, and perhaps he was simply looking for an excuse to wreak havoc on the farm regardless. When Minna informed the Zulu that the only other adult in the house was Fritz's Uncle Jan—an elderly, near-blind gentleman who posed no physical threat whatsoever—the Zulu began to make physical threats towards Minna. In the corner of the room, a young Fritz watched on as the warrior physically berated his mother, seemingly helpless to save her.

However, without any hesitation, Fritz silently manoeuvred his way towards the Zulu's assegai spear, which he'd placed against a nearby wall. Without any noise whatsoever, like a shadow leaping from the darkness, Fritz thrust the warrior's own spear directly through his midsection. His stomach exploded in a heaping mass of blood and torn flesh. The unimaginable agony and incredible shock at being attacked by a child sent the Zulu falling to the floor, writhing about in pain as blood shot out onto the farmhouse's wooden floor. He pulled in desperation to remove the spear from his chest but only managed to break the spear in half, leaving it embedded in his torso. Within a few seconds, the warrior lost consciousness.

Minna couldn't believe what had happened. Her young, innocent son had willingly taken the life of another human and had done so with such ease that it was more than a little concerning.

'You've killed him!' she screamed at Fritz, unable to comprehend the reality of their situation. After a few minutes of shock, Fritz embraced his mother in an attempt to comfort her. He apologised for being so impulsive but made sure that his mother knew he didn't regret his actions. He began to cry, but only out of sympathy for his mother's mixed emotions.

'I wasn't frightened,' said Fritz, 'but I did feel funny.'

The following year, when Fritz was only thirteen years old, he boarded the Kamerun steamer, which carried him to mainland England. It was a completely different world from what he had become accustomed to. No longer did he have to be constantly prepared for Kaffir or Zulu invasions or have to hunt for meals with his father. Instead, he was sent to an affluent private school in the heart of Oxford.

The lifestyle change was not Fritz's idea. He'd even fought against his parents' wishes for his better life overseas. He found it difficult to leave his parents behind in South Africa, especially during such turbulent times, but he adhered to their requests and availed himself of a proper education.

It was here that Fritz's competitive nature became fully realised. He immersed himself in every British sport possible—football, rugby, wrestling, boxing—and found an exhilarating sensation in besting British boys at their homegrown games. Aside from sports, he was an outstanding student, excelling in all manner of academic subjects. During school holidays, he returned to South Africa to spend a small amount of time with his family, before returning to Oxford to continue his education.

In England, Fritz experienced his first taste of romance with the daughter of a local priest. A young girl named Elspeth, already married, showed great interest in Fritz, unsurprising given his natural good looks and athletic figure. The two began an affair together that lasted until Fritz left the school at age 16.

Many sources state that Fritz Joubert Duquesne enrolled in studies at Oxford University following the successful completion of his high school studies. However, like so much of Fritz's life, it is difficult to ascertain whether such rumours are true. It is true that Fritz's father and uncle encouraged him to pursue further academic studies, but whether Fritz did or not is a different story. It is believed that between the ages of 16 and 20, Fritz travelled Europe (with the occasional jaunt back to South Africa) to acquaint himself with as many of the fairer sex as possible. His affair with Elspeth had given him a taste of what true satisfaction felt like, and so Fritz consciously sought out romantic liaisons wherever possible. Despite what little we know about Fritz Joubert Duquesne, one thing we can say for sure is that he considered himself something of a ladies' man.

According to Fritz's own account, he enrolled at the prestigious Ecole Militaire, a military academy based in Brussels. It was here, Fritz claimed, that he acquired his vast knowledge of military equipment, explosives, engineering, and weaponry.

If Fritz's claims are to be believed, he would have enrolled at Ecole Militaire around 1898, which was at a time when the strain between the Boers and the British in South Africa was approaching its inevitable breaking point. War was on the horizon, meaning it was possible that Fritz had every intention of joining the battle and so began training at Ecole Militaire to ready himself. Around this time, Fritz received a message from his father pleading with him to return home. Abraham wished his son to take part in the upcoming Second

Anglo-Boer War. Fritz complied with his father's requests, and so made his way to Hamburg and then on to Pretoria, South Africa.

Chapter 2: The Man Who Hid The Kruger Millions

War finally broke out in 1899, for which Fritz Joubert Duquesne offered his self-proclaimed military expertise to the Boer commandos. He was quickly awarded the rank of lieutenant, which eventually progressed to colonel. During October of the same year, it appeared that the British forces possessed more power and tactical mastery than their South African counterparts, and so laid claim to a handful of victories as the first few Anglo-Boer battles were fought. Initially, British forces assumed that the Boer commandos would pose little threat to their established military operation, and up until 20th October, 1899, their assumptions were correct. The British achieved victory at Mafeking, Talana Hill, and Elandslaagte, but their success was short-lived.

A Boer victory came on the trails of Nicholson's Nek, a contested territory that the British had begun to cover, expecting an easy victory to arrive shortly. However, the Boers managed to steal a victory, much to the shock of British forces. This would be the first of three separate victories on the same day. Within a matter of hours, Boer forces also claimed Lombard's Kop, a small hill in the east of Ladysmith. It was in this battle that Fritz received his first war-inflicted scars, suffering a bullet through his shoulder at the hands of a British infantryman. A simple, common wound, yet one Fritz would gladly boast of for the rest of his life, often embellishing the tale of how he acquired it. It was a wound that he found brought him respect in the company of his peers and sympathy in the company of the opposite sex – sympathy he could then use as a catalyst to more illicit activities.

Boer victories gradually increased in number. No longer was their success considered to be a stroke of good fortune, instead attributed to the military prowess displayed by the South African forces. The year of 1899 saw many significant victories for the Boer commandos, and this would also be the year that Fritz Joubert Duquesne's first appearance in the history books would come about. The South African president at the time – President Kruger – fled the capital in the wake of the war for the purposes of his safety. He took with him his men, his family, and of course, his riches. Sources vary on the exact value of the gold that President Kruger attempted to carry, but it's estimated to be somewhere between the value of one and five million pounds.

It had been Kruger's intentions to transport the gold by carriage across South Africa and onto the Delagoa Bay railway to transfer it to Europe and keep it safe from the British invasion. However, with British troops beginning to make a presence across several European cities, Kruger considered it too dangerous an endeavour, as the railway lines could easily fall into British hands at any time. Therefore, Kruger decided to cart the gold via carriage to the coast, where a vessel would be waiting to collect it and take it to Europe.

In total, around thirty wagons were loaded with goods. However, there were additional wagons—decoys—deployed by Kruger to fool the British army. Some wagons contained gold, some wagons contained legal paperwork, and some wagons contained nothing. Even if the opposition *did* manage to thwart their efforts, at least some of the gold would find its way to the coast. Each wagon was sent out in a different direction and at different times to ensure the best chance of a successful trek. The driver of each wagon had been instructed to meet at a secret rendezvous spot in Transvaal (the northern lands of South Africa), where more of Kruger's men would take over.

However, several miles into the initial trek, Duquesne interjected himself into the operation. For reasons that remain unknown, Duquesne commandeered authority over all the wagons using credentials he claimed were given to him by President Kruger himself. Kruger, Duquesne claimed, had written a letter instructing him to oversee the entire operation.

In reality, it seems incredibly unlikely that President Kruger would delegate such a task to such a young, inexperienced military officer, but it seems that Duquesne's persuasion techniques were particularly effective in all sorts of circumstances. However, given that President Kruger had been indecisive about how exactly to go about hiding his millions, it is plausible that he would employ an overseer. Very shortly, all the cart drivers believed that Fritz Joubert Duquesne was to lead them to their intended destination.

Fritz sent half of the wagons (the ones with no gold aboard) to Maputo, East Africa, and personally oversaw the journey of the other fifteen through the South African wastelands. It soon dawned on Duquesne that the people he was travelling with were unaware of exactly what goods were loaded inside each wagon. Allegedly, President Kruger hadn't informed the trekkers of what lay inside due to fear of theft or worse. However, the haulers soon discovered that they were in the presence of millions of pounds' worth of gold. For the following two weeks, Duquesne and fifteen other men trekked deeper into the vast South African territories, hundreds of miles away from civilization. Amongst the haulers were four white men, and it would be these white men who made the rookie mistake of trying to outsmart Fritz Joubert Duquesne.

Between themselves, the white men hatched a plan to assassinate the other haulers, starting with Duquesne, to keep the riches for themselves. However, Duquesne learnt of their plans from a fellow South African hauler and so set in motion his plans to stop them.

One evening, Fritz loaded up his sleeping bag with clothes and rags to give the illusion he was sleeping. That same night, one of the white men approached the sleeping bag and plunged a knife deep inside. However, all he was met with was a handful of cloth.

From the shadows, Duquesne fired a bullet directly into the back of the head of his attacker, killing him instantly. His shots caught the attention of the others, in response to which Duquesne shot three more bullets into their backs. They all fell to the ground while a startled group of Kaffirs looked on in terror.

With the conspirators out of the way, the Kruger gold was Fritz's for the taking. Under his command, he ordered the remaining Kaffirs to take the riches towards the Drakensberg Mountains in the South. Once there, he made them unload the gold by hand deep into some nearby caves. There, it would remain for over a century.

A problem soon dawned on Fritz—he wasn't the only person who knew where the gold was hidden. He also had to worry about ten other people. If any of them were captured, they could possibly reveal the location to the opposition in exchange for their freedom. Similarly, a stroke of greed could overcome them, and they might return to the scene to extract the riches for themselves.

Therefore, Fritz devised a deceitful, albeit ingenious, method to address his problem. He had become aware that his men had taken a liking to some of the women holed up in a nearby kraal. Some of the villagers had also noticed and responded with aggression and threats towards the Boers. One evening, once all the gold had been dispatched, Fritz visited some of the gentlemen in the nearby kraal and, according to his own claims, convinced the villagers to attack Fritz's own settlement.

Sure enough, two nights later, the natives attacked their camp, killing all of Fritz's men. They disposed of their wagons, their supplies, and their personal possessions, leaving no trace whatsoever of them behind. By this point, of course, Duquesne had already made his escape into the night.

Fritz Joubert Duquesne had made a clean getaway. As far as he knew, he was the only person on earth who knew the whereabouts of President Kruger's gold. Exactly what Fritz planned on doing with the gold—or even why he performed this arduous task—remains something of a mystery. He never returned to collect the riches, nor did he inform anyone of their location after the war. It has since been theorised that perhaps Duquesne simply stashed it there so that he could collect it once the war was over but forgot due to other circumstances that befell him. It's also been theorised that Duquesne planned on returning to the site to claim the gold for himself once the dust of war had settled.

However, another theory poses the idea that this was simply the first of many fabricated myths about Fritz Joubert Duquesne that would collect over the years.

Chapter 3: Captive of Sin

Duquesne returned to his Boer unit, his foray into thievery never to be mentioned again. It is unclear whether he interacted with President Kruger following his theft (or even before his theft), leaving conclusions about the incident entirely to the collective imagination.

Around this period, Fritz established himself as something of a freelance saboteur. He found himself in Barberton, South Africa, along with many of his fellow Boers. However, at this point, Boers had begun to fight without specific units. There was no central command and no hierarchy of officers. Instead, it was every man for himself, the only thing uniting them being their ethnicity. Gone was the security of an established commando unit, and in its place, the constant fear of capture or attack, with the former being much more likely.

It was while on the run in Barberton that capture first became a reality for the young Duquesne. Imprisonment was to become commonplace over the course of his life, but it was his first capture that really forced Fritz's desperation and internal terror to reveal itself.

While Fritz and a handful of other Boers were being transported to a labour camp, Fritz seized an opportunity for escape when he found himself in the company of a lone guard. In the blink of an eye, he grabbed the guard's gun and shot him in the head without pause or hesitation. Fritz and the other prisoners immediately fled the scene, heading back into the war-ravaged lands of Barberton for another shot at freedom. Unfortunately, this freedom would be short-lived, for Fritz at least, as he quickly found himself a prisoner again following his hasty trek into East Africa. This time, he had been shot at in the head, a bullet narrowly missing his brain. Fritz fell to the ground, lost consciousness, then awoke to find himself at the mercy of a British patrol.

But once again, escape wasn't far from his mind.

As he was being marched into a prisoner of war camp located in Vrede, Fritz analysed his surroundings and realised that a brute-force approach would be a bad idea in his circumstances. Unlike his previous capture, there were more guards than he could count surrounding him. Therefore, he was going to have to employ a different approach if he wanted a successful escape. This time, he decided to adopt the con approach.

He began speaking to one of his jailers as though they were old friends. Fritz was nothing if not persuasive, and soon found himself establishing a kind of perverse rapport with one of the men trusted to guard him. He hung at the back of the group, chatting away to his jailer on all manner of war-related topics. Then, as he and his fellow prisoners were being taken across a bridge covering the Klip River, Fritz attacked the man he had so effortlessly chatted with during his journey towards imprisonment. The guard fell to the ground, his sudden collapse drawing the attention of everyone around them.

However, before they could register what had happened, their first visual was of Fritz Joubert Duquesne leaping over a wooden railing and down into the crystal waters of the Klip River. Whether it was an impulsive manoeuvre or one he had planned beforehand remains unknown, but it was a ballsy move either way. Fritz landed into the icy cold waters and swam for safety without looking back. His hands had been shackled by his captors, and so Fritz swam using what little movement his limbs were allowed. When he reached a small clearing, he looked back, seeing silhouetted figures peering from the bridge above. He hadn't heard anyone jump after him, but the sound of gunfire and hysterical voices echoed in the shadows behind. He waited until the sounds subsided, then used the surrounding rockery to cut loose his ties. He was a free man, but he was a wanted man. This marked Fritz's second escape from British forces, making him a sure target of their subsequent operations.

Fritz made his way across South Africa towards Swaziland. Everywhere he turned, the results of Lord Kitchener's scorched earth policy were to be found. To deny the opposition any resources, intelligence, or security, Kitchener had commanded that every village, every town, and every settlement be burnt to the ground. South Africa had become a barren dead zone of nothing but the charred remains of homes and the occasional roaming wildlife.

In Swaziland, Fritz was quickly taken as a captive for a third time. Within days of entering the territory, Portuguese officers apprehended him, as their location was considered to belong to the British forces. Fritz was correctly deemed to be a member of the opposition. Once again, he was restrained and marched towards the nearest railway tracks. He was stuffed aboard a crammed train and dispatched almost fifty miles to the nearest British labour camp. There, he was thrown into a damp prison cell littered with dirt and rats, while the overbearing stench of sewage seeped in from a nearby drain. His conditions were horrific, even for a prisoner of war—therefore, Fritz quickly masterminded an escape plan.

He wasted no time in carrying out his plans. On the first evening of his imprisonment, Fritz managed to claw his way into a ventilation shaft on the ceiling of his cell. He waited until the midnight hours, when everyone assumed he would be sleeping, and clambered atop his furniture to make his escape. He removed the ventilation grate slowly and silently, then pulled himself to the lightless passageway between the prison ceiling and the roof. There, he made his way along the entire length of the prison towards an opening. A barrier of rusted guardrails blocked his exit, but Fritz forced his way through them.

However, once he made his way past the guardrails, he found himself in another area of the prison entirely. Through another shaft below, he saw a room full of guards and no escape in sight. He traversed along the dim passageways in the ceiling trying to find anywhere he could safely lower himself and escape through more conventional means, but Fritz was quickly heard and recaptured by a group of guards.

Realising that the man they'd apprehended on the roof of their jail was the same man who had escaped their clutches twice already, the British deported Duquesne to Lisbon, Portugal. There, he was placed in a high security prison camp where escape would be next to impossible.

Yet, in a stroke of luck that only Fritz Duquesne's luck could conjure, he found the opposite to be true. His Portuguese jail was almost a comfort to him, given his recent months of hardship. He discovered that the Portuguese jailers weren't aware of his status as a multiple escapee. Fritz quickly built up a friendly rapport with his Portuguese jailer. Whether this was through Duquesne's manipulation tactics or whether his jailer just naturally took a shine to him is debated amongst researchers, although the truth is likely a combination of the two. On the authority of this particular jailer, Fritz was given special privileges that his fellow captives were not. Unlike the other prisoners of war, he wasn't confined to his cell for 23 hours a day, and instead was allowed a reasonable amount of freedom around the prison grounds, both indoor and out. On occasion, he was allowed to roam around the outskirts of the prison under the watchful supervision of two guards. This allowed him to gain a reasonable understanding of the prison layout including, mostly importantly, the walls that would lead to his eventual escape. He was even allowed to converse with other prisoners on occasion, most of whom were his countrymen.

As always, freedom was at the forefront of Fritz's mind. On a starless evening in the autumn of that year, Fritz happened across a young woman named Donna Joanna wandering the grounds of his Lisbon prison. The two struck up a conversation, from which grew a great affection, eventually progressing to lovemaking. Donna eventually revealed to him that she was the daughter of Fritz's friendly jailer, which not only shocked Fritz but also gave him ample opportunity for a convenient escape. After many illicit rendezvous in various parts of the prison facility, Fritz told Donna that he couldn't remain holed up in jail for much longer. His country needed him, and he needed to extract vengeance on those he detested. Surprisingly, Donna sympathised with his cause. Fritz asked her not to inform her jailer father of his intentions, as it would surely hinder him further.

Through vague promises of togetherness that Fritz had no intention of keeping, he used Donna's affection towards him to allow him access to the outdoor grounds of the prison out of sight of the guards. Once there, he fled hastily over the prison walls and out into the Portuguese night, promising to meet up with Donna when the dust of war had settled. In true Duquesne fashion, he left Donna that same night and never returned, perhaps leaving her waiting for the rest of her life.

The following morning, when the friendly jailer went to check on his captive friend, Fritz Duquesne was nowhere to be found.

Chapter 4: A Lifelong Hatred

Fritz Duquesne's intentions were to return to the war, but his slew of recent captures had dissuaded him from fighting the British directly. He fled to Europe in search of Dr Leyds, a representative of Transvaal, located in Brussels, Belgium.

He found Leyds and told him of his recent hardships and lucky escapes from three different British camps. Leyds advised Fritz to flee the war altogether and take refuge until the war had ceased, especially given his reputation as a magician-like escapist. Leyds informed him that upon his next capture, the British might not be so forgiving, and might instead simply kill him where he stood. Despite this, Fritz had no intention of hiding away. He was determined to fight the British head on in any way possible. This was when Dr Leyds suggested the idea of infiltrating the British army from within. According to Leyds, Fritz could offer his services to them under the guise of a Boer defector. He could begin working at their military camp, then gradually progress his way to field work. Fritz did exactly that.

Aldershot, England: This was the British army's central military camp, which held the vast majority of British infantry and weaponry. Gaining access to the British military was simple enough for Fritz, although details of what transpired are not a matter of public record. Instead, we can only assume that his charm and persuasion worked in his favour. During the second Anglo-Boer war, it was quite common for a Boer to swap sides and fight against his own countrymen. These men were referred to as 'Judas Boers' by their compatriots. However, many farmers and villagers didn't care who won the war as long as it soon ceased. Many South Africans just wanted to return to their normal lives, which would happen as soon as the fighting stopped. Whether their land fell under British or South African ownership wasn't a concern to them. However, it was a dangerous tactic, as a Judas Boer would be executed immediately if they encountered their countrymen who hadn't abandoned their cause. With Lord Kitchener soon being appointed as the new commander-in-chief of the Anglo-Boer war, he quickly assembled these Judas Boers into their own division and sent them all out to fight on the frontlines. It was a backhanded tactic, one which pitted Boer against Boer, and whatever the outcome, British lives would be saved as a result.

After two weeks at the Aldershot encampment, Fritz was awarded the rank of lieutenant and sent back to South Africa to fight against his countrymen. This was exactly what Fritz wanted—however, he had no intentions of killing any fellow Boers. The only ones who would die by his hand were the people who assumed he was one of them: the British.

It was now March of 1901. All across South Africa, farm burning had become commonplace, leaving thousands of families homeless and without food, aid, or shelter. These families were left to wander the vast wastelands of the South African veld, living hour by hour, not sure when the next meal would present itself. To combat such conditions, the British set up camps throughout South Africa to offer refuge from the hazards of war-induced conditions, but this well-meaning gesture quickly turned into something else entirely. With limited supplies available, thousands of South African families travelled to these camps with expectations of food and medical assistance—regardless of how minor—but quickly found there was none to be had. Instead, they sat alongside their fellow homeless natives and waited for death. With such an influx of starving, downtrodden people holed up together in one place, disease quickly spread among those present, increasing the death rate at an alarming pace. Instead of sanctuaries away from the war, these British camps slowly evolved into concentration camps. As far as the Boers were concerned, this was exactly what the British wanted to happen. It wasn't, of course, but it was difficult for the Boers to see otherwise.

Fritz had been appointed as part of a military operation to cross South Africa and erect a series of barbed wire fences to literally trap the remaining Boers inside. Such an operation was considered inhumane even by the people employed to carry out the task, but it was nevertheless effective.

However, once Fritz arrived on South African soil, he had found himself drawn elsewhere. He made his way back to Nylstroom, the location of his old family farm. Until now, he hadn't found an adequate opportunity to return to his homeland to be reunited with his family. Similarly, he hadn't seen or heard from his mother, his sister, or his uncle in over a year. Naively, he had assumed them to be safe. After all, the British would have no need to rid them of their homes. They ran a simple farm trade, nothing more. His mother was an old woman now, and his sister barely out of her teens. His Uncle Jan still lived with them, too. By now, Fritz assumed, he would have become fully blind. They posed no threat to anyone. He expected them to still be around, perhaps waiting with open arms for their heroic relative to return, but this would not be the case.

When he finally arrived at the patch of land where his family farm once stood, he found only a smouldering mound of charred remains in its place. The whole Duquenne farm had been reduced to ashes since he'd been gone, and he hadn't even been aware of it until now. There was a familiar smell in the air: the stench of burnt flesh. In a moment of panic, Fritz feared that perhaps his mother, sister, and uncle had been burnt alive inside their home. However, on closer inspection, Fritz discovered that the smell was of charred livestock, not human remains. A small relief washed over him, but it did nothing to quench the overwhelming sensation of panic and rage rapidly building inside him. He had questions that needed answering. Where were his family? Were they alive? Had they relocated elsewhere?

Fritz scoured every inch of the farm looking for a clue as to what might have happened to his relatives. Eventually, he found a hole dug into the burnt earth. As he burrowed inside, he found that it was the entranceway to an improvised bunker, effectively concealed from view. Inside, he met with a gentleman named Kanya, one of the men who had worked on the Duquenne farm for several years. When the British arrived to lay waste to the farms of Nylstroom, Kanya began digging the bunker in preparation for the inevitable destruction. Unfortunately, it seemed the bunker had been uncovered by the British, and whatever was inside had been extracted and dealt with accordingly. Kanya likely made his escape prior to such horrors, but then returned when the British had moved on. Kanya claimed that he knew Fritz would return home one day, and would, therefore, wait to tell him of what truly happened.

The reality of what transpired was worse than anything Fritz could conjure up in his imagination. At the very worst, he expected to hear of the quick, albeit unnecessary, death of his family. However, as Kanya began to describe the horrific ordeals his family were needlessly subjected to, Fritz felt his deep hatred of the British swell to unquenchable levels.

First, his Uncle Jan: according to Kanya, Jan had been beaten, restrained, and then hanged from a telegraph pole. Around the time of the Anglo-Boer War, hanging as a form of execution was designed to induce strangulation as opposed to snapping the neck of the captive, which was what had occurred in the case of Uncle Jan. As he felt the oxygen drain from his body, Uncle Jan had been attacked with bayonets while his limp body swayed in the spring winds. It was a death without dignity. A blind man needlessly tortured by military officers who, for no other reason beside sadism, had gone beyond their duty to inflict death on an innocent civilian.

When it came to Elsbet, his beloved sister, Kanya told Fritz of the sexual assault she had been forced to endure at the hands of five ruthless infantrymen. Allegedly, Elsbet had been restrained by three officers while two others watched to make sure she couldn't escape. One by one, each man took a turn raping her while she cried out for mercy on the ground, all of the men ignoring her pleas in favour of laughing at her misfortune. How many times she was raped remains unknown, but at the very least, three British officers had their way with her, likely in front of other civilians and military personnel.

Once the men were finished with Elsbet, they let her go and pushed her away from them, instilling in her a minor sense of hope that she may survive. They all watched as she fled into the afternoon sun, but her departure was quickly cut short. As the group of men laughed, one of them shot her in the back. Elsbet fell to the ground, dying on the spot. They had given her hope, only to inflict even further despair.

Despite the circumstances, there was an element of completion to the tale of Uncle Jan and Elsbet. He knew the facts, regardless of how horrific they were. They were dead. They couldn't be saved. They were gone, and they couldn't come back.

However, when it came to his mother, it was a story without a conclusion, which then infuriated Fritz even further. Kanya informed Fritz that he had seen Minna flee the scene without clothes, suggesting she had also been brutally raped at the hands of the British military. He heard her cries and saw ropes dangling from her hands, suggesting that she had also been restrained prior to her sexual assault. Although she had been barbarically attacked, she had not been killed. Instead, a handful of officers had led her away. To where, Kanya didn't know, although Fritz had an idea. The first thought that crossed his mind was that she had been sent to a nearby concentration camp for labour purposes.

The nearest concentration camp was Germiston, located around ten miles outside of Johannesburg. Without hesitation, Fritz made his way there. It took him several days to reach it, but he gladly abandoned his military duties in favour of finding his mother. He didn't care.

Using his lieutenant credentials, Fritz informed the guards there that he urgently needed to speak to a woman by the name of Duquenne. They didn't have her name to record, but Fritz told them he would scout the grounds for her.

He passed through rows of dead, dying, and diseased captives: old and young, male and female. Guards had informed him that an outbreak of syphilis was running through the camp, and so Fritz would need to take precautions not to come into contact with the infected. He didn't care. His only aim was to find his mother.

Inside a barbed-wire enclosure, Fritz found the woman known as Minna Duquenne. She had been reduced to a skeletal figure, completely malnourished, her skin having taken on a sickening yellow hue. In her arms, she cradled a young child barely one year old. How she acquired the child is unknown—it may have even been her own produced from the sexual assault at the hands of a British guard. Both Fritz's mother and her mysterious child were suffering from syphilis, likely contracted by their close proximity with other infected prisoners.

His mother was mostly unresponsive, her state of mind having deteriorated to the point of ruin. However, Fritz leaned down to his mother—despite the hazards involved—and whispered his final words to her:

'As long as I live, I will never draw one breath but to pay back the English for what they have done. Most of all, Lord Kitchener, who had done it, who had ordered it, who had planned it. I pledge my soul that for every drop of rotten, poisoned blood in your body, I will kill one hundred Englishmen.'

Fritz turned his back on his mother, knowing that this would be the last he would ever see of her. They would meet again in death, but that day was a long way off. As he made his way out of Germiston, Fritz nodded his salutations in the direction of two guards. They returned his gesture, but once their backs were turned, Fritz pulled out his pistol and shot both soldiers in the back of the head.

Fritz approached their motionless bodies and kicked away at them in a fit of rage. It was an act that would be symbolic of the next fifty years of his life.

Chapter 5: Cape Town Betrayal

Maximum destruction was Fritz Duquesne's primary aim, and where better to wreak such havoc than in the British central hub of South Africa, Cape Town?

It was October of 1901. Along with a group of trusted informants inside the British army, Fritz had orchestrated a destructive scheme designed to inflict damage that would cost his enemies dearly. With this plan, Fritz was certain that a Boer victory would be inevitable.

Although Cape Town was highly contested territory in the early stages of the war, it had quickly been claimed by Lord Kitchener's troops. Now overrun with British troops, its extensive railways and sizable harbour provided perfect conditions to handle shipments of weaponry and personnel. There were few Boers to be found in Cape Town, as their presence would quickly be noticed, and they would soon be captured or killed. The only South African residents in Cape Town were refugees who had requested the assistance of the British in keeping them alive during such chaotic times. Most were British sympathisers who longed for the end of the war, and so believed that siding with the British would be the path of least resistance. In truth, such refugees didn't care which side won the battle but assumed that the British had a distinct advantage given the size of their operation. Therefore, siding with them gave them the best shot at survival.

Although Cape Town was a significant location of the Anglo-Boer War, it had somehow managed to maintain its economy. Unlike its neighbouring cities, Cape Town did not show signs that it had been the scene of a fierce battle. Its buildings remained intact, and many of its residents strolled around as though there were no war going on. Perhaps the most noticeable difference from pre-war Cape Town was that the residents were greatly outnumbered by wandering refugees. It was difficult to find a bridge, a storefront, or an alleyway that wasn't crowded with starving families or unlucky lone vagrants.

By evening, Cape Town adopted a different aura altogether. The rich banded together to visit theatres and hotels, worlds apart from the horrors endured by those not a part of the wealthy elite. The general opinion of the upper class was that the Boers stood little chance at victory, and therefore silently sided with the British.

Meanwhile, it had taken Fritz Duquesne months to assemble a trusted team of confidantes to execute his strategy. One by one, he approached Boer defectors inside the British army and used his persuasion skills to discover the truth regarding their intentions. It turns out there were many like himself: Boers who wanted to bring down the British from the inside. The same people believed that a Boer victory would be difficult without such backhanded tactics. Likewise, there were many defectors who still prayed for a Boer victory but sided with the British due to their sizable advantage. In life or death scenarios, cultural heritage was often forgone in favour of prolonged survival.

Fritz spent several months planning the attack with twenty other Boer sympathisers. On the night of Friday, 11th October, over a hundred explosives would be strategically placed at major British vantage points across Cape Town. These included personnel encampments, ammunition depots, power plants, railway lines, bridges, government buildings, public buildings, and anything else the British might deem useful to their cause. Even places such as the Cape Town Opera House—a place often overflowing with the wealthy and upper class—were not spared in Fritz's extreme lust for vengeance. At its core, Fritz's actions were a response tactic to Lord Kitchener's scorched earth policy. If the British were burning down anything in sight, then Fritz would respond with the same aggression and ruthlessness. He would literally fight fire with fire.

Setting off multiple explosives at once would not be an easy feat. It would require masterful precision and coordination between Duquesne and his associates. Therefore, as insurance against the possibility of failure on the part of his helpers, he assigned the most important task to himself: the destruction of the water pipeline located at the peak of Table Mountain.

Through this pipeline ran thousands of tonnes of water every single day. In total, somewhere in the region of fifty-million gallons of liquid could be expelled from the pipeline, providing enough damage was caused to it and water to the pipeline wasn't cut off at any point. To damage the pipeline to the extent Fritz planned would eventually unleash every single drop onto Cape Town—situated 3000 feet below the point where the explosion was planned. The initial explosion would cause all water within to furiously crash down onto the city, no doubt destroying anything in its path. As more water flowed through, the force would then push the water through the city, causing a tsunami effect across South Africa's most prestigious city. At the same time, other explosions would cause further chaos, eventually resulting in the obliteration of the entirety of Cape Town. Only those who were aware of the plans would be spared. Fritz knew that he would be taking the lives of thousands of innocent civilians, refugees and Boers alike, but it was a necessary evil on the path to destroy his enemies.

On the evening of Friday, 11th October, their plan was to place the explosives at midnight, followed by their detonation in the early hours of the morning. The reason this date was chosen was due to the fact that many British military officials would be attending a dinner in the heart of Cape Town, allowing for maximum slaughter. In true Fritz Duquesne style, he also made his presence known at the dinner party, attending in full military regalia as a way to mock his unassuming peers. However, his demeanour was somewhat different from usual. Gone was the persuasive, charming Fritz Duquesne, and in its place was a sombre, focussed Fritz concerned only with the upcoming act of large-scale vengeance. Many beautiful women approached him but, very uncharacteristically, he made his excuses and removed himself from the conversation. Women were not a priority on this evening—perhaps for the first time in his life.

But at 9 p.m. that evening, all of Fritz's plans would come to an end. In a lavish banquet hall with hundreds of British officers in attendance, a lone gentleman tapped the British governor on the shoulder. He whispered something into his ear. Many eyes in the room watched their interaction, correctly assuming that everything wasn't as it seemed. Fritz sat alongside five of his associates, doing his best to maintain his aura of tranquillity.

But that was when everything changed.

Unbeknownst to Fritz, one of his associates had betrayed their entire cause. Although the gentleman was a Boer defector who harboured similar tendencies to Fritz, he had come to realise the severity of his intentions. When he considered that the entirety of his homeland would be lost, he had suddenly suffered a change of heart. At the very last minute, he had informed military higher-ups of their plans and spared no details doing so. He gave them names, plans, and exact locations. They knew everything. Their game was over.

The governor returned to the room then made his way directly to Duquesne. Trying his best to be inconspicuous, he tapped Fritz on the shoulder and requested his presence in the hallway outside. Immediately, Fritz feared the worst.

'You're under arrest, Lieutenant,' said a British officer alongside the governor, 'for conspiracy against the British government.'

A panicked Duquesne reacted in the first manner that came to him. He pretended as though he had no idea what the officer was talking about. Governor Hely-Hutchinson took Fritz's side momentarily. The governor was aware of Fritz's status as a Judas Boer but believed he was fully committed to fighting for King and country. In a state of disbelief for both Fritz and the governor, Fritz Duquesne was shackled and taken to a secure prison in Cape Town. His vengeance had been foiled, this time by one of his own countrymen. If the rage inside him hadn't already reached breaking point, then this act ensured that it would.

Chapter 6: Professional Manipulator

Despite the governor's pleas, Duquesne received no sympathy. Realising that he was out of his depth—at least for the time being—Fritz followed the orders of his captors. He was placed under the watchful eyes of three British troops and taken to Cape Castle the following morning to await sentencing.

With the severity of his crimes quickly commanding the attention of British military higher-ups, Fritz Duquesne's trial was set for the following morning, only two days after his plans were foiled. He spent his first evening in Cape Castle staring idly from his concrete prison cell out into the distant waters of the South Atlantic sea. The prison was an ancient fortress built centuries prior, and its two-inch thick walls and twenty-foot high perimeters ensured that escape was virtually impossible, even for the Houdini-like Fritz.

In the adjacent cells sat Fritz's nineteen fellow conspirators, all of them awaiting the inevitable news that they would be put to death. These were not the first traitors to be uncovered within the British army during the Anglo-Boer wars—far from it. At least thirty men suspected of treason had already been captured and sentenced since the war began two years before. Some were granted life imprisonment, but most weren't so lucky.

The following day, Fritz and his nineteen companions were marched to the courtroom inside Cape Castle. They were assigned a basic military defence team consisting of a mid-ranking colonel and an official legal representative, but their plea for innocence fell entirely on deaf ears. Their guilt was obvious the moment the whistle blower was summoned for questioning. He spilled the details of their planned deceit, sparing no details whatsoever.

The informant, a Judas Boer himself, told the court that he betrayed Fritz's operation out of fear of losing his land, his property, and what few of his loved ones remained during their siege on Cape Town. Following his official confession, the judge turned his attention to the defendants. He asked them individually whether they had anything to say in their defence, but every one of them, including Duquesne, shook their heads.

Some did so with a look of vengeful determination in their eyes, some with a look of sorrow and regret. Fritz, however, did more than simply confirm his guilt. With all the Hollywood theatricality he would later become known for, he stood up to address the court and spoke out with earnest honesty:

'All of the charges are true,' he said. 'That, and much more.'

The judge questioned him regarding his boastful statement, but Fritz first attempted to plant some seeds of doubt in the minds of his captors.

'Other than the man who just testified, I have never seen these nineteen men before in my life,' said Fritz. 'There were nineteen others as part of my plan— but they are not these defendants.'

While his comments were overlooked by the judge, they were certain to have stirred up suspicion in the minds of the British military officials in attendance. It was Fritz's way of instilling the idea that there were more Judas Boers amidst the British infantry ranks, as well as a desperate attempt to award his co-conspirators an ounce of freedom.

The judge's response was to accuse Fritz of being a 'traitor'. However, Fritz stood his ground. He realised that a death sentence would undoubtedly be handed to him, and so used his final moments to inform the British officials in attendance exactly what he thought of them.

'I have not failed one day in this uniform to send out word to my own people of what the British were planning—right down to the last detail. Traitor? I have been the most faithful Boer in all of Africa.'

Fritz's uncharacteristic honesty caused the generals in attendance to respond with great hostility. Many officials interrupted his speech with calls of his immediate execution for not only severe sabotage, but for his blasphemy towards the British military.

'Your commanding general—the vilest bastard spawned in hell, the blackest, most poisonous soul that ever befouled the earth—has swept my land clean of cattle, property, and resources. He has burnt all of the fields, all of the houses—my own amongst them. At General Kitchener's orders, my own sister was raped and killed by three British soldiers.'

From the rear of the court, a general opposed Fritz's statements, claiming that such barbarity was not a part of Kitchener's orders. The rape and murder of his sister were merely taken upon by the soldiers themselves—Lord Kitchener had no control over their actions and certainly didn't encourage it. However, Fritz paid no attention and continued his rousing speech.

'My blind uncle, who had never harmed man or beast in his life, was hung by jeering soldiers. My mother was raped, impregnated, and infected with syphilis. She now lies moments from death in a concentration camp, nursing her unwanted bastard in her arms. The little I have done to

England so far is nothing to what I will do before I am through.'

Without any hesitation in his body, Fritz directed his words at the British generals surrounding him.

'For what this land did to my mother, I will wreck that bastard country, that bastard empire, right to the last foul inch of its stolen possessions. For my mother's violated body, I will send your daughters to the stews and your sons to the torture chamber. And for Kitchener himself ...'

Fritz's blasphemous words were cut off by the full force of a British general's fist connecting with the side of his face. Fritz fell to his chair and then toppled to the ground. Few rushed to his aid, fearing even further repercussions from the court. As Fritz composed himself, the general and legal counsel confirmed their sentencing decision with a brief nod of their heads in each other's directions. Their decision was unanimous and took only a matter of seconds to arrive at.

'The sentence of the court is that these nineteen men be shot at sunrise. Fritz Duquesne is to be given a dishonourable discharge from His Majesty's forces, and that he be shot at sunrise after witnessing the death of his accomplices. May God have mercy on the souls of all of them.'

In a span of two days, Fritz Duquesne and his band of co-conspirators had been betrayed, uncovered, trialled, and sentenced. In twelve hours, they would be executed on the grounds of Cape Castle and given a dishonourable burial at sea.

Yet, in the early hours of the following morning, mere hours before their death sentence was to be carried out, the general arrived at the door to Fritz's prison cell.

'May we talk?' he asked.

Fritz didn't respond to him, instead using the short amount of time he had left to figure out a way to save himself from his fast-approaching demise.

From the other side of the iron bars, the general said:

'You do not have to die.'

Duquesne maintained his silent demeanour and let the general say what he had to.

'You say you have been in touch with the Boers during your time with us. You must know that occasionally, Boer coded messages fall into our hands. You must know these codes.'

It was clear what the general wanted, but Fritz's loyalty to his people prevented him from obliging the general's request. However, this didn't mean he couldn't use the situation to his advantage.

'If you die at sunrise,' the general continued, 'how can you aid your Boer cause?'

'What do you expect from me?' asked Duquesne.

'The complete Boer codes. Tell us the codes, and I give you my word that your life will be spared. You will receive nothing worse than life imprisonment.'

After several minutes of intense contemplation, Fritz finally gave his answer.

'I accept,' he said. 'I will not die at dawn.'

True to the judge's demands, Fritz was marched out of his cell at sunrise to witness the slaughter of his nineteen co-conspirators. One by one, the men were shot at execution range and unceremoniously piled together for transportation to the bottom of the seabed. Following this massacre, Fritz was taken to the general's office to translate the first of many Boer dispatches. Fritz did so. However, by the time the British would discover that the codes he had given them were completely fake, Fritz would be long gone.

Chapter 7: A Bid For Freedom

After narrowly avoiding a death sentence, Fritz Joubert Duquesne was now fated to spend the rest of his days concealed within an impenetrable concrete fortress on the South African shores. He had relayed the Boer codes to his captors, who would then use them to translate any messages they could intercept from their opponents. However, such processes would take time, meaning British officials hadn't yet realised that the codes he supplied were completely made up.

Two weeks into his lifelong prison sentence, Fritz began to take the steps to free himself from Cape Castle. He spent his days staring out into the South Atlantic waters from a raised cell, with only a bed and a bucket to keep him company. Unlike the previous jails he had been locked in, there was very little chance of him befriending a naive guard or slipping out into the courtyard without supervision this time around. Fritz knew that escape from a fortress of such magnitude would take significant time, and so put his plan into action as soon as circumstances allowed.

Duquesne positioned his bed slightly below his cell window to conceal his activities. He told his jailers that the new positioning would allow him to fully enjoy the breeze from the Atlantic Ocean, and fortunately for Fritz, his jailers didn't question his motivations.

In similar fashion to his escape from imprisonment in Swaziland the previous year, Fritz began to gradually dig away the mortar holding the bricks of the fortress together using a metal dinner spoon he had stolen during meal time and concealed beneath his bed. Each night he would spend hours scraping away the walls, then discard the cement dust through the gap between cell bars. It took him almost three weeks to loosen the first brick, but as more mortar fell away, his job became easier with each brick removed.

Two months later, he had finally tunnelled his way to an opening. In the early hours of a winter morning, Duquesne pushed each of the loosened bricks outward, away from his cell. Each time he pushed, he waited until he heard the thud of the brick connecting with the outside ground before continuing, fearing that pushing too many bricks out at once would cause a loud crash that would draw the attention of the prison guards.

Fritz squeezed through the small hole on his back until the scent of outside air enveloped him. Just as freedom was within reach, a large brick—loosened by Fritz's removal of the ones beneath—fell from above and pinned him in the small gap. The constricted conditions meant that Fritz couldn't gain any leverage to push the rock off his chest. He couldn't move. The outside world was only a few metres away, but Fritz could only lie helpless inside a makeshift tunnel in Cape Castle's walls. He was trapped. The only way he would survive was if Cape Castle guards pulled him to safety.

Within minutes, consciousness faded. If it hadn't been for the fact that Fritz had attempted escape in the early hours of the morning, he surely would have died that day.

Fortunately, prison guards were on the scene within a few hours. They dug out Fritz Duquesne's lifeless body and sent him to British doctors for medical assistance. He was lucky that his ribs or spine hadn't been crushed, but he had suffered a handful of severe internal injuries that would affect his day-to-day life for the next few months.

Once his health had been ascertained, Fritz was placed in inescapable shackles and sent to solitary confinement. Following several threats of being executed for attempted jailbreak, British officials eventually decided to deport Fritz to the Bermuda Islands where he would remain in a similar maximum-security facility. Additionally, Fritz

Duquesne was given an instruction that only further fuelled his hatred of the British.

'Under order of the banishment proclamation, you are to be perpetually excluded from South Africa. Under no circumstances will you ever be allowed to return.'

Banished from his own country for crimes against the regime that sought to claim the land for their own. It was a punishment, an insult, and a motivation all at once. With more than a hint of sarcasm, Fritz simply said:

'Thank you.'

On November 7th, 1901, Fritz Duquesne was marched through Cape Town's bustling streets in shackles and chains. His destination, the Cape Town dock, was where he would board the ship *Harlech Castle* headed for the Bermuda shores. Before he was shoved aboard, British soldiers carried out two further insults to an already irate Duquesne. Firstly, they ensured that Fritz's restraints were as tight as physically possible around his wrists, arms, and ankles. Since his reckless escape into the Klip River, they knew that no possibility was too extreme for Fritz Duquesne. The scars left as a result of these restraints remained with Fritz until the day he died.

Secondly, British soldiers held Fritz down and removed every strand of his brown flowing locks. This infuriated Duquesne, as he had made a silent promise to himself that he would not cut his hair until the Boers had been awarded freedom.

Alongside more than three hundred of his countrymen, Fritz Duquesne was forcefully pushed below deck to the holding cells where he would spend the next seven weeks.

The *Harlech Castle* set sail for Bermuda. Behind him, South Africa gradually disappeared from view until it became no more than a memory. This was the last time Fritz Duquesne would ever see his homeland.

Conditions aboard the *Harlech Castle* were treacherous enough to drive many prisoners insane. During the forty-five day trek, all prisoners were given the bare minimum food to survive: raw oats for breakfast, one mug of tea or coffee, and then soup in the evening. Holding cells were vastly overcrowded and littered with dirt, grime, and vermin. There was a constant din twenty-four hours a day, not only from the struggling prisoners but from the British soldiers on deck who found it amusing to provoke and harass the prisoners on board. The unbearable conditions drove many to madness. Some took their own lives by jumping overboard when they were allowed briefly on deck each day.

As always, escape was not far from Duquesne's mind. He would make two attempts during the journey, but neither would be successful. In the first attempt, Fritz and a handful of other prisoners planned to abduct the ship's captain in the middle of the night, overpower the British soldiers, and steer the vessel towards the shores of Europe. However, as with his Cape Town destruction plot, his plans were leaked to the British officers on board by a mole within their group.

That same day, Duquesne and his band of ambitious prisoners-of-war were escorted to the *Harlech Castle*'s equivalent of solitary confinement: a handful of lightless, freezing cell blocks with conditions twice as bad as the general barracks. For several days, they were given nothing but water to sustain themselves, had no blankets, and were made to sleep on the cold, damp ground.

After thirty-three days, the *Harlech Castle* made a stop at the Azores to collect supplies. While there, Fritz attempted a second escape, this one a lot more reckless and impulsive. When he and his fellow prisoners were brought up on board for fresh air and exercise, Fritz noticed a rifle placed atop a small barrel. When Fritz looked around, he saw a disinterested guard talking to a handful of prisoners around thirty feet away. He assumed that the guard had left his post and subsequently forgot his rifle along with it.

In the blink of an eye, Duquesne picked up the rifle and launched himself towards the distracted guard. From behind, he cracked the guard on the back of the head with the butt of the gun, killing him instantly. The prisoners looked on in horror; partly out of shock, partly out of concern for Fritz's punishment when he was inevitably caught. However, Fritz was a man who lived in the moment. He didn't have time to think about what would happen—he only concerned himself with what *could* happen.

He disposed of the guard's body overboard then made his way to an area reserved for British troops. Once there, he quickly positioned himself inside a hawsehole—a small passageway used to pass through a ship's anchor—and remained there for as long as he could. His plan was to slip out in the middle of the night when searches for Duquesne had been called off (and likely he would be presumed to have jumped overboard) then swim back to the Azores shore. However, his plan was foiled within one hour.

'Come out, you bastard, or we'll fill you full of holes,' shouted a British soldier. Fritz remained in place for several minutes, but a narrowly-dodged bullet let him know that his captors weren't prepared to take mercy on him. Reluctantly, he pulled himself out, shook off his cramp, and surrendered himself to his captors. He was placed back in solitary, this time with even more restrictions than previously. Two more weeks went by before the Harlech Castle pulled into Hamilton Harbour in Bermuda.

Although his ratio of successful to unsuccessful prison escapes was by no means equal, at this point in his life, Fritz Duquesne had successfully escaped imprisonment three times. Very soon, he was going to add one more to the list.

Bermuda, as beautiful as it was with its golden sand and crystalline waters, was considered to be on the same level as Alcatraz regarding the likelihood of any of its inmates escaping. Only a handful of ambitious prisoners had ever dared escape from the island— including a fellow Judas Boer whom Fritz had travelled with on the Harlech Castle. While the man in question was apprehended the moment he reached dry land, other escapees were not so lucky, with all of them having drowned or been eaten by sharks.

Seventeen thousand prisoners of war arrived on the Bermuda Isles the same week as Fritz. The place was not a prison as such, but a concentration camp where these Boers would be put to manual work to aid the British colonisation of the place. Barbed wire fences separated Fritz's designated island into three territories: the Royal Engineer's workshop located at the centre, the general prisoners' barracks at the southern end, and the reinforced enclosure for troublesome prisoners at the northern part of the island. Naturally, Duquesne was immediately banished to this last zone for his actions aboard the Harlech Castle.

Before he could seek freedom, Fritz knew that he needed to commit the layout of the island to memory: every guard outpost, every fence, every building. He claimed to the guards that his name was Fritz Jean du Quenne, claiming his origin country as Belgium, but that he was an American citizen. Reasons why Fritz might have lied about his heritage are many, but a fake identity awarded him two advantages: when he inevitably escaped, he would be more difficult to track down, and it also obscured his history as a Judas Boer.

One of the punishments for the prisoners in the special enclosure involved them being restrained for a minimum of fourteen hours a day in tight-fitting, unforgiving shackles with zero leeway. Fritz's wrists were joined directly together with no chain between them. The guards assumed that if a prisoner was unable to move his arms, swimming away would be impossible.

But Fritz Duquesne would eventually prove them wrong.

The barbed wire fences and perimeters of the island did not allow for simple navigation. Many areas were indistinguishable from others, often confusing the layout of the island in the minds of potential escapees. Fritz had already witnessed one prisoner attempt a daring escape over a barbed wire fence into what he believed to be open water, only to be caught in more barbed-wire fencing on the other side. Similarly, another prisoner successfully made his way to the Bermuda shore but was met with further barbed-wire restrictions once he dove beneath the water's surface. When the guards pulled the would-be escapee from the water, Fritz saw the man's torso had been significantly lacerated.

This would be another obstacle in Fritz Duquesne's already impossible task, but he was not deterred in the slightest.

Many months passed—enough for Fritz's flowing brown locks to grow back to at least shoulder-length. It was on June 25, 1902, that he departed his prison-island for good and made his fourth successful jailbreak in less than three years. On a night soaked by heavy rainfall, Fritz slipped through a loose panel holding up the barbed wire perimeter. Fritz had no master plan in mind, nor did he employ any human manipulation of any kind. It was the most basic escape of Fritz's criminal career—he simply fled the area and prayed that fortune was in his favour.

With his clothes safely tied around his waist and neck, Fritz leapt into the shark and barbed-wire infested waters and began the two-mile-long journey to the distant coast. Lights from cruising patrol boats came within a hundred yards of him, but Fritz silently submerged himself beneath the water long enough to evade detection. He was unsure which direction to go, but an occasional beam of light flashed from King's Point lighthouse in the distance, which Fritz used to guide himself towards the mainland.

His ninety-minute long swim was a treacherous one, with midnight currents sweeping him far from his intended destination. Luckily, the lighthouse beam was visible even from two miles to the east, meaning he was eventually able to find land following a rigorous swim against the violent waves. On multiple occasions, Fritz needed to submerge himself below the waters to avoid light beams from the Bermuda watchtowers, as well as to hide from what the British referred to as 'guardian angels', the patrol boats that constantly sailed the island perimeter.

But by some miracle that only Fritz Joubert Duquesne could pull off, he found himself scaling the rocks towards dry land with two miles of sea separating him from his prison island. Once more, freedom was his.

Chapter 8: Independence

Fritz knew that his notoriety as a Judas Boer and British rival would prevent him from making any significant advances towards his enemies, at least in plain sight. So, ever the trickster, Fritz decided to establish a completely new identity far away from the contested territories of the Anglo-Boer War. His detest for the British certainly hadn't faded. However, his infamy would not bode well in his favour. Revenge would come in time, and that would have to be enough for the moment.

Upon his return to civilisation, Fritz enlisted the help of a notorious Boer sympathiser named Anna Maria Outerbridge. Her home, located in Bailey's Bay in Bermuda, was something of a sanctuary for fleeing Boers across the country. Clearly a wealthy woman, Anna Outerbridge was a high-ranking member of the Boer Relief Committee who spent her time assisting Boer forces in any way she could. Fritz initially found shelter in her home for a short period.

Outerbridge noticed that the streets of Bermuda were rife with patrolling British forces—more so than usual—suggesting that they had deployed a significant number of personnel to track down the missing Duquesne. Following his stay at Outerbridge's Bermuda home, Fritz Duquesne returned to civilisation with a new haircut, new clothes, and most importantly, a new identity.

Now residing in Hamilton, Bermuda—albeit mostly in the shadows—Fritz set about making money any way he could. His goal was to slip on board a vessel headed for America with enough coin in his pocket to sustain him during his first few months there. Once there, he would continue his destructive efforts towards the British and their land.

Fritz, a clear man of the world, knew full well that the easiest way to make money was via the oldest profession in the book. While he could attract the fairer sex with relative ease on a personal level, foray into the male prostitution world was not an idea Fritz was willing to entertain. Therefore, he enlisted the services of a local prostitute named Vera for whom he would act as an intermediary. Fritz would scour the local taverns and bars for willing gentlemen and charge them six shillings for an evening in Vera's company. It was a fair price, and much lower than the going rate for local prostitutes in the area. Fritz would then split the money between himself and his sultry colleague before retiring to shelter at a local motel each night.

Over the ensuing weeks, Fritz amassed more money than he'd known in his short life. Now in his late twenties, Fritz considered the idea that maybe city living was a life more suited to his tastes. It seemed he certainly excelled in sales and persuasion—despite the unsavoury industry he was currently working in—and certainly these skills would translate to other areas of work.

However, heading towards such a lifestyle would be a step in the opposite direction from his life's goal. He might be able to provide a comfortable living for himself, but his desire to eradicate the British would go unfulfilled. Although he was a man of deceit, Fritz Duquesne was also a man of morals. He wouldn't give up on his cause yet.

In addition to making a substantial income, Fritz's position as a pimp awarded a secondary advantage: access to information. Fritz instructed Vera to question her clients on their business nature, and it was no surprise that many of her midnight gentlemen were members of the British forces. Vera would then obtain information regarding vessels setting sail for the United States under some vague assertion about wanting to move there to be with her family. This information would be relayed to Fritz, who then assessed the likelihood of his being discovered if he boarded the vessel in question.

It was in early July when a gentleman named Tomkins enquired with Fritz about using the services of his colleague. Naturally, Fritz obliged and brought the two together. Before Tomkins and Vera engaged in their illicit affairs, the three shared several drinks together in the corner of a dimly lit Hamilton bar. They were four whiskies into their conversation when Tomkins revealed the reasons for his presence in Bermuda. He was actually a sailor aboard the ship *Margaret*, which was en route to Baltimore, Maryland. It had docked at Bermuda for re-fuelling and would be out of action for at least five hours, and so the crew had descended upon Hamilton for their own personal re-fuelling. To many crewmen, this involved the company of ladies of the night.

Tomkins had no idea that his statement had just ensured him a very eventful evening, and not just because he would soon be locked away behind closed doors with the beautiful Vera.

Fritz plied Tomkins with alcohol to the point that reality became a blur. Once he was suitably intoxicated, Vera took Tomkins to a back room and began the deed. Before she closed the door, she waved goodbye to Fritz Duquesne and silently thanked him for his short-lived assistance. Fritz returned the gesture, then put his plan into action.

While Vera and Tomkins made love, Fritz commandeered Tomkins' sailor uniform and headed towards the docked ship *Margaret*. There, dressed in his erstwhile companion's clothing, he boarded the ship with ease. Security measures were somewhat lax, particularly during the early hours of the morning when many returning sailors were more than a little worse for wear.

The *Margaret* set sail for Baltimore within twenty minutes of Fritz's feet touching the deck. A new chapter in Fritz's life was on the horizon. Once he was safely in America, his enemies would be thousands of miles away, meaning the threat of capture and imprisonment would no longer haunt his every step. He could be reborn as someone new and find a different way to exact vengeance upon the regime who murdered his family and scorched his homeland.

However, adventure was never far away. Before he reached America, there would be one more obstacle he needed to overcome.

Before the sun rose the following morning, Fritz's true identity as an escaped prisoner of war was uncovered during a routine headcount of sailors on board. Fritz knew that, by this point, the *Margaret* had already travelled enough miles for a return journey to Bermuda to be a significant waste of time. Instead of the ship turning around and dispatching Fritz from whence he came, he would be taken to America, albeit in shackles. However, he had been in enough restraints in the past that such a threat no longer concerned him.

Fritz was marched into the captain's quarters and forced to explain himself to Captain Witer. Witer, more concerned with the fact he had lost a steward than having a stowaway aboard his ship, greeted Fritz with great hostility.

His first accusation towards Duquesne was that he had killed Tomkins in Hamilton and stolen his uniform. However, Fritz assured Witer that he had merely plied Tomkins with alcohol until he passed out.

'To hell with the Boers and your escape stories,' responded Witer. 'When we reach Baltimore, I'll turn you over to the immigration authorities and you'll be sent right back to South Africa. I should throw you in the brig, but thanks to your little scheme, I'm a steward down. Get to work.'

It was clear that once Fritz reached America, he wouldn't be a free man as he had hoped. Captain Witers would turn him over to immigration officials in restraints, and he would either be deported or imprisoned. His only option was to flee the *Margaret* before it reached dry land, although this wouldn't be an easy task under the circumstances. There were no more drop offs or refuelling points on the way to Baltimore. It was a direct three-day journey. He would need to leap overboard once the shores were within reach, then make his way to the mainland alone.

It only took one day for Fritz's desperation to reach boiling point. Less than 30 hours following his unannounced arrival on board the *Margaret,* Fritz saw an opportunity for escape when the ship passed along the shores of Chesapeake Bay. At the closest possible point, he slipped over the ship's railings, lowered himself as far as possible towards the water's surface, then projected himself away from the ship and down into the Atlantic Ocean. There was a great risk involved in making such a jump, particularly from a ship as large as the *Margaret*. Too little force, and he would succumb to the currents created by the vessel's underside rotator blades, which would drag him below the surface and crush his body with little effort.

Fortunately, he escaped such a demise due to a masterful dive that launched him just out of the rotator blades' radius. As he looked up from the icy waters, he saw a handful of fellow prisoners peering over the railing, likely having witnessed the whole thing. The *Margaret* sailed on towards Baltimore as Fritz kept himself as invisible as possible below the water's surface until it was safe for him to swim outward. He expected flashlights to be shone in his direction, perhaps even sailboats coming to recapture him, but neither came. Once the ship was a reasonable enough distance away, Fritz swam towards the shores of Chesapeake Bay.

In a moment of irony, as Fritz stepped foot on the Baltimore mainland, the date ticked over to the 4th of July, 1902.

Chapter 9: A Different Life

The exact circumstances of how Fritz Joubert Duquesne went from hardened Boer soldier to New York journalist is not so much a mystery as it is widely disputed. He certainly *did* go from soldier to writer, but the journey Fritz travelled to get there is still debated by Duquesne researchers.

From Baltimore, Fritz railway hopped until he found himself on his way to Paterson, New Jersey. He sustained himself with the money he had earned during his brief stint as a pimp but wasn't opposed to stealing and scrounging if the conditions allowed. Once in Paterson, he called upon the assistance of Boer sympathisers whom Anna Outerbridge had put him in contact with. One such sympathiser was a gentleman named Richard Weightman, who also happened to be an editor at the *Washington Post*. Weightman had previously been a reporter during the start of the Anglo-Boer war and published many anti-British pieces in the *Post*, allowing him to become one of the most prominent Boer advocates in the whole of America. Naturally, he took a great shine to Duquesne following his stories of tragedy and triumph, and made a great effort to assist Duquesne in making a life for himself in America.

With Weightman's help, Fritz managed to land a low-paying position as a subway conductor for a meagre $20 a week. He worked this position for several months before requesting Weightman's assistance again in increasing his earnings in any capacity. Eventually, he found a job as a subscription collector for the prestigious *New York Herald*, although it paid only $5 a week more than his subway conductor position.

Still, it was advancement, and at the moment that was all Fritz could ask for. His day-to-day activities involved close relationships with journalists and newspapers workers, and it seemed that everyone he struck up conversation with was fascinated by his tales of war-time hardship. Indeed, Fritz's life story is still considered a unique one to this very day, so at the time, it must have sounded like a work of fiction. While a few of Fritz's colleagues did indeed take his stories with a hint a scepticism, his ability to enthral his listeners was second to none. Even if some people didn't believe his stories, they were more than happy to hear them told in the mesmerising fashion of which he was capable.

Fritz's stories eventually caught the attention of the editor of the *Sun* newspaper, a gentleman named George

Mallon. Although he was reluctant to leave behind the people who gave him his first opportunity in America, his new friend Richard Weightman was also a regular contributor to the *Sun*, and Fritz was even encouraged by Weightman to join their ranks. Fritz did so and used his new opportunity to tell his life story on a grand scale. His story-telling ability clearly translated well to the written word, as reactions to his tales were overwhelmingly positive. Many people regarded him with sympathy, and many vicariously acquired Fritz's detest of the British through his stories of unnecessary cruelty inflicted upon his mother, uncle, and sister. It is worth noting that many of these publications are what biographies of Fritz's life base their facts on, which is where inconsistencies in his life story originate.

This remained Fritz's life from 1904 to 1906. He was promoted to Sunday editor of the *Sun*, where he remained for another year before moving to other New York newspapers: The *World* and the *Herald*. Journalism gave way to playwriting, and this evolved again into novel writing. All his outlets were greeted with admiration and success, rewarding Fritz Duquesne with a healthy lifestyle and enough money to live one rung above comfort.

By 1909, Fritz Duquesne had amassed wealth, prominence, and a fulfilling career. It was difficult to believe that only 10 years prior, this was a man fighting on the frontlines across war-ravaged South Africa. Now, he was settled in a modern country, having already had the experience of more than a hundred people combined, and making a healthy living in one of the most prestigious cities in the world.

And yet, this wasn't enough for him. Despite these incredible achievements, Fritz still had only one burning desire inside him. Success and admiration may have sufficed in the short term, but it was not a complete substitute for his goal of vengeance against Lord Kitchener's army. By now, the Boer war was over, but Fritz still took every opportunity he could to declare his hatred of the British. Now his audience was drastically larger than anything he'd known before, so he received correspondence from hundreds of people sympathetic to his cause.

Messages came from all parts of the world; from British civilians themselves right up to high ranking political figures. One of these figures happened to be the most senior politician in the whole of America: the President of the United States.

Theodore Roosevelt, the twenty-sixth American president, had initially been intrigued by Fritz's stories of heroism on the South African frontlines. However, when he discovered that Fritz was also an accomplished hunter, Roosevelt's interest in the man was truly piqued. It was an article about big game hunting that led Roosevelt to contact Duquesne. The piece read:

Like most Boers, I have been hunting since I was ten years old. Danger and hair breadth escapes have happened so frequently to me that most of my hunting experiences appear almost too commonplace to record. It would be impossible to hunt any length of time in Africa and without having some adventure worth relating. Adventures in which a steady eye, nerves of steel, and a brain as quick as lightning are life-saving essentials to a big game hunter.'

It was 1909, and Roosevelt's second term as president was coming to an end. As a middle-aged man plagued with health issues, it was not a stretch to believe that Theodore Roosevelt didn't have much life left in him (a fact confirmed by his death at age 60). His big game hunt across South Africa was intended as a retirement gift to himself, and by his own words, he was as excited 'as if I were a boy'. To provide himself the most genuine experience possible, he requested the presence of Fritz Duquesne—or the 'Boer ivory hunter' as he referred to him—at the White House in January 1909. Without any hesitation, Fritz accepted the offer despite his being aware of

Roosevelt's position on the Anglo-Boer War. Roosevelt was not a Boer advocate by any means and went as far to say that it was *'essential to African welfare that England win the war'*. While he also claimed that he did not approve of many of the British's actions, he also didn't discourage them. However, despite the circumstances, a man of Fritz's ego would not turn down an opportunity to assist the President of the United States.

Despite being a wealthy politician, Theodore Roosevelt was as passionate about South African hunting as any would-be adventurer Fritz had come across in the past. For two hours, Roosevelt questioned Fritz on everything that came under the umbrella of big game hunting. Fritz was more than happy to impart his knowledge of firearms, ammunition, animal weak spots, the best African hunting grounds, and the most efficient way to skin certain species to the president. Soon, the conversation turned to Roosevelt's frail condition, with Fritz remarking that while he admired his ambition, Roosevelt may be somewhat underestimating the harsh conditions of the South African outback. He told Roosevelt: 'You may prefer to be taken to game preserves where the game is plentiful and tame.'

Roosevelt retorted in typical fashion. 'I'll have none of that,' he said. 'I want to take a hunter's chance. I want to shoot game where it is most dangerous.'

It was clear that he had done his homework. Roosevelt astounded Fritz with his knowledge of South African terrain, topography, and geographical restrictions. He also possessed an incredible array of hunting equipment, with Fritz later claiming that Roosevelt referred to his rifles in the same way a proud parent would refer to their child.

It was a brief meeting, but one which served Fritz's career as a respected journalist and novelist well. He returned to New York to continue his writing career, offering his services to a handful of newspapers in the area to report on his meeting with the now ex-president. Much to the surprise of everyone, Fritz did not praise Roosevelt's decision to go hunting, instead choosing to approach it with a negative spin. It may have been a manipulative tactic to garner more readers, or Fritz may have genuinely believed that the former President was making a big mistake in venturing into the wild in such a fragile state. Fritz may have also seen this as upper class privilege coming into play. There was no doubt that Roosevelt would be surrounded by experienced hunters who would jump in to save him should there be an issue Roosevelt couldn't handle on his own. Duquesne never had such a luxury during his hunting expeditions with his father. If an elephant charged them, they would need to act fast or die. Roosevelt, on the other hand, had more than enough security to ensure his survival.

Will Roosevelt Return Alive? was the front-page headline of the March 1910 issue of *Travel Magazine.* In the article, Fritz praised Roosevelt's determination but blasted his final decision. Fritz made the claim that it was unlikely Roosevelt would return without at least some significant injury or disease— a claim which was confirmed upon Roosevelt's return to the USA. He had contracted malaria during his time in Uganda and suffered with it until his death ten years later. It is likely to have been a significant factor in his early demise.

Duquesne and Roosevelt remained acquaintances for the next several years. In 1912, Roosevelt ran for the presidency one more time despite his age and health, and Duquesne rallied in his favour all across the country. In 1914, Roosevelt convinced Fritz to assist him on an expedition across South America. Duquesne was incredibly reluctant to do so but figured it would not be much of a hardship considering Roosevelt's current condition. Up until this point, Fritz had continued his career in literature and begun a lecture circuit around America. Additionally, he had married a woman named Alice Wortley, with whom he had become acquainted during his time in South Africa, having rekindled the relationship overseas.

Alice accompanied Fritz and Roosevelt on their foray into the South American wilderness, but a sudden turn of events would quickly put an end to their merry expedition.

While Fritz was serving as Roosevelt's shooting instructor across the isolated terrains of Brazil, Fritz's most despised enemies had just declared war on Germany.

If there was an opportunity to exact revenge on the British, Fritz would be the first in line.

Chapter 10: War, At Last

Surprisingly, it was not Fritz Duquesne that offered his services to the German forces, but the other way around. No doubt his tales of British sabotage had reached overseas shores thanks to the wide reach of New York newspapers, meaning British foes were well aware of his burning hatred for their enemies, not to mention the apt skills that Duquesne claimed.

A directive from German forces was issued in winter 1914 requesting the assistance of all overseas agents who might be willing to help their cause. It is unclear exactly how Fritz received this direction during his time in Brazil. It may have been that he was contacted prior to the initial frenzy of war outbreak. The directive stated:

> *It is indispensable by the intermediary of the third person having no relation with*

the official representatives of Germany to recruit progressively agents to organise explosions on ships sailing to enemy countries in order to cause delays and confusion with loading, the departure and the unloading of these ships.

Upon receiving the news, Fritz employed a ruse to separate himself from Alice. Roosevelt had already progressed through the jungle at a much more rapid pace than his less-enthusiastic colleagues, therefore his presence would not be an issue. Alice, however, had allegedly only feigned interest in the expedition from the start. She didn't want to be there, nor did her levels of enthusiasm correlate well with the harsh conditions forced upon them. Therefore, Fritz told Alice that she should return to New York, and he would continue the expedition alone. He informed her that the conditions ahead would require an even greater level of endurance—a level that only experienced adventurers were capable of. It didn't take long for Fritz to persuade Alice to leave his side, and so the pair made arrangements for her departure. Once Alice had returned home, Fritz began his new operation.

Exactly why Fritz was opposed to informing Alice of his true intentions is unknown, although it was likely due to confidentiality reasons. His directive was to be covert, and the more people familiar with his actions, the higher the likelihood of his being discovered. Furthermore, Alice was a liability. He would not put it past his enemies to abduct his wife for use as a bargaining tool or worse. Therefore, the less involved she was, the safer it was for them both.

From the Brazilian jungle, Fritz made his way to the east coast and then on to Venezuela and Nicaragua. Almost overnight, he had gone from acclaimed author to undercover infiltrator. As though a light switch had been flipped, Fritz switched his personalities like an Oscar-worthy actor: from scholar to saboteur. Gone was Fritz Duquesne and in his place was either George Fordham, Piet Niacoud, or Frederick Fredericks, each alias with a convenient backstory to suit whatever situation he found himself in.

Fritz's first stop was the watering holes of whichever South American territory he found himself in. His modus operandi consisted of chatting to sailors who worked aboard the English vessels carrying cargo across the Atlantic. From them, he would not only extract information regarding their intentions, but would offer each of them bribes for a small favour. It was a life not dissimilar from his Bermuda pimping days, albeit with a completely different goal in mind. While Fritz's physical characteristics lent themselves more towards Eastern European heritage, his many years in the USA awarded him a perfect American accent. The partnership between the USA and UK had already been established, so

English sailors were willing to give Fritz the benefit of the doubt.

His ruse was to inform his newfound sailor companions of his invented backstory, in which Fritz claimed to be a botanist. He would then offer them a small fee to smuggle a small box of orchids on board their ship. The box, Fritz claimed, could then be mailed to one of Fritz's relatives once it reached English shores.

Of course, there were no orchids. However, there was a box, but inside were tightly-packed explosives that Fritz believed could sink any vessel they detonated from. When social deceit wasn't an option, Fritz also claimed to have placed explosives aboard docked ships himself, although such a feat would require levels of manipulation perhaps even Fritz Duquesne was incapable of. This particular method has been debated by researchers over time, and it's highly unlikely it occurred. However, Fritz famously recounted such tales in later life with great attention to detail.

Whether Fritz's claims are true or not, it cannot be denied that many British vessels fell victim to sabotage on the icy Atlantic waters during this period. How many Fritz was responsible for is unknown, but he later claimed to have successfully sunk at least twelve.

Ever the storyteller, Fritz did not only weave tales of his success in this time, but also claimed that he had narrowly escaped capture on at least two occasions. The first saw him engage in a physical battle with a British soldier who discovered Fritz loading cargo onto a stationary vessel. As it wasn't a large ship, Fritz couldn't claim he was one of the on-board sailors, as he wasn't a familiar face. Instead, he fought off the soldier, incapacitating him with his firearm and likely leaving him for dead. On another occasion, Fritz claimed to have had his true identity discovered by an officer with whom he had previously engaged in the British army. The soldier rallied the troops to take down Duquesne, but he skilfully manoeuvred his way across the rooftops of a Brazilian port town and out of their clutches.

This told Fritz that, while he may have reinvented himself in the short term, he could not keep this ruse up for long. British intelligence were already aware of his antics during the Boer war and likely attempted to keep a watchful eye on him in New York. However, once they realised that Duquesne no longer resided in the country he had called home for twelve years, they connected the dots.

It would be on 21st February, 1914 when Fritz's identity as a German spy was blown.

Along with an accomplice named Bauer whom Fritz had befriended during his dive bar crawls, he planned the sabotage of a prestigious vessel named the Tennyson. The ship's intended destination was Liverpool, England, and on board were an array of military supplies, raw minerals, and dried coconut kernels, called *copra*. It was a simple plot, and one which researchers later found surprising that Fritz didn't employ more often.

Fritz, or George Fordham as he was known during this excursion, loaded up a large wooden crate of what he told authorities were film negatives. With a fake shipping address written on the surface, Fritz requested that the box be delivered with utmost urgency to New York (the Tennyson's first drop-off destination). Whether or not there were indeed film negatives inside the box remains unknown, but the deafening explosion in the middle of the sea later that day suggested there weren't. The blast took the lives of three people on board, with seven more receiving significant injuries that would last the rest of their lives. A great fire spread across the wooden vessel within minutes, but those who avoided the blast managed to calm the fire with hundreds of buckets of sea water frantically thrown across deck. As the vessel rocked on the fierce Atlantic sea, waves helped to douse the flames until the captain could regain control. He steered towards the nearest dry land and ensured he and the remaining sailors escaped to safety.

Following their report, investigations into the source of the explosion moved quickly. From the onboard manifest, British intelligence traced the blast back to Fritz's co-conspirator Bauer. Bauer was arrested in Brazil, and Duquesne's name and aliases were soon extracted from him.

They knew his name, they knew his aliases, and they knew what he looked like. Given his notoriety as both a literary scholar and a hardened war criminal, it would be more difficult than ever for Fritz to operate only from the shadows. This didn't dissuade him, of course, but this little setback made his life infinitely more difficult. Fritz needed freedom, and he needed discretion. He was now wanted for murder charges and for conspiracy with German operations —in addition to what he considered the 'minor' charges of sinking and burning British ships, destruction of military stores, warehouses, and coaling stations, and the falsification of documents.

He spent several days considering his options. He was now holed up in South America with an entire army searching for him. Outside of his espionage efforts, Duquesne was currently in talks with an Argentinian production company to produce several educational films. It was a project that would have netted him an incredible sum of money, and despite his current predicament, it was an opportunity he didn't want to lose. Making the crossing between Brazil and the USA via conventional means would surely result in his capture.

In the impulsive mind of Fritz Duquesne, there was only one option that remained.

Chapter 11: A Necessary Death

The headline read: CAPTAIN DUQUESNE IS SLAIN IN BOLIVIA.

> *Captain Fritz Duquesne of New York, noted adventurer and soldier of fortune, has been killed in a battle with Indians on the Bolivian frontier. His expedition was looted by the attacking band.*

According to a *New York Times* journalist, the great Fritz Joubert Duquesne was no longer a threat to the British Empire. The piece had been picked up by the *New York Times* following a story in a smaller New York publication by an unheard-of journalist. The story told of Fritz Duquesne's trek into the South American jungles alongside Alice Duquesne and Theodore Roosevelt. Allegedly, Fritz had returned there with camera equipment to document Roosevelt's expedition, but an altercation in Bolivia had robbed him of his life. The story said that under other circumstances, the great adventurer may have stood a chance against a group of tribesmen, but the harsh conditions he was subject to beforehand reduced him to a weakened state.

Of course, this was all completely untrue. The author of the original piece was Fritz himself. If he were dead, the British would put a halt to their search for him, giving him a much better chance of passing across the United States border safely. It didn't entirely ensure him impunity, as surely the British were wise to Fritz's antics by now, but it certainly increased his odds significantly.

Via a German vessel, Fritz returned to America undiscovered by his enemies. It could be argued that he had engineered the perfect circumstances for an undercover spy to thrive. He was considered dead by everyone other than his wife and close confidantes, meaning he could simply assume another alias, alter his image, and take on a completely new identity. However, in a true Duquensian twist, an article published twelve days following his obituary returned the deceased Fritz back to life.

> *CAPTAIN DUQUESNE FOUND WOUNDED: WILL RECOVER.*
>
> *Captain Fritz Joubert Duquesne of New York, explorer and soldier of fortune, who was in command of an expedition into the Bolivian wilds, has been found by troops at Rio Pilcomayo in a badly wounded state, after a battle in which his expedition had attacked and defeated a band of Indians on the Bolivian frontier. Aid was sent to the wounded explorer who is expected to recover.*

Indeed, he could retroactively blame lazy journalism on his brief death, but the reasons why Fritz decided to return to life are one of the biggest mysteries plaguing Duquesne researchers to this day. It would have been understandable if he had resurrected himself following excessive British sabotage to return to a normal life, but he remained dead for less than two weeks. With his speedy resurrection, the worldwide manhunt for him immediately resumed.

The answer may lie in simple convenience. As a legally deceased man, there would be certain restrictions in place in regards to everyday activities, in addition to legal implications for Alice regarding their possessions and assets.

On the other hand, it may have simply been that Fritz's ego wouldn't allow him to operate from the shadows. In his previous life he attacked his enemies directly, infiltrating their ranks and personally overseeing their demise. It seems that Fritz Duquesne needed his enemies to know it was he who caused them to fall.

Between 1914 and 1916, Fritz devised an elaborate scheme that was incredibly bizarre even by his standards. Despite having accrued a hefty sum of money during his years as a literary scholar, it seemed that he wasn't quite satisfied with the amount he had stashed away. This was largely out of character as Fritz never seemed concerned with wealth, providing he made enough money to survive. However, with the possibility of the Great War spreading to America, he may have been collecting enough money to see him through a long period of dormancy.

Duquesne completed the educational film commissioned by the Argentinian production company, for which he was paid $24,. This was a considerable sum of money at the time and likely would have sustained Fritz for several years, even in New York. The reels for the film were stored in a Brooklyn warehouse, although they legally belonged to the Bueno Aires Board of Education. Sometime in May, 1916, an anonymous gentleman going by the name Frederick Fredericks allegedly insured the film for $33,000 with a New York-based insurance company.

As it happened, mere weeks after the insurance was put in place, the warehouse containing Fritz's film reels burned to the ground.

Investigations into the incident uncovered that according to a night watchmen who worked there, a man fitting Duquesne's description had attempted to break into the warehouse one evening. When the watchman halted his attempts, the man offered the guard a bribe to look the other way for one night only. When the guard refused, the would-be criminal fled the scene.

If one insurance scam wasn't enough, Fritz also had another iron in the same fire. Two years prior, Fritz had been responsible for the wreck of the *Tennyson* ship on the Atlantic high seas. Fritz claimed that negatives for the same film were aboard the *Tennyson*, and that they were worth somewhere in the region of $80,000.

Of course, authorities were well aware that it was Fritz Duquesne who knowingly sabotaged the *Tennyson* and did so with his supposed own high-value materials on board. It was an incredibly bizarre, brash move that was almost too surreal to believe. He committed seven criminal acts the day he detonated a bomb on the *Tennyson*—including crimes punishable by execution – and now he was requesting compensation money as a result. It was a strange, almost unbelievable move, and one highly out of place for Fritz Duquesne.

At this point in his life, Fritz may have been deeply contemplating his future, which would go a long way to explaining his strange behaviour. The First World War had already been ongoing for two years and showed no signs of stopping any time soon. He may have been attempting to procure enough money to provide Alice with a comfortable life without him, or likewise, may have seriously considered the possibility that he may be a casualty of war if he continued his reckless ways (as he intended).

On the other hand, the entire operation could have been a master plan that ultimately fell apart. As Fritz hadn't been seen in public since his resurrection announcement in the New York press, many assumed that he was indeed still dead, a fact later proved by the Stuyvesant Insurance Company, who investigated the circumstances around the torched Brooklyn warehouse. In their efforts to ascertain the truth, investigators could not prove who Frederick Fredericks was, or if indeed he was the same person as the notably absent Fritz Duquesne. Furthermore, exactly why such a person would insure an item under a false name—not to mention an item of which their connection was tangible—made for all around suspicious circumstances. The whole situation reeked of a scam, and when Stuyvesant Insurance Company couldn't even prove if Frederick Fredericks or Fritz Duquesne were even alive, the claim fell flat. It is possible that the whole thing, including the bizarre *Tennyson* insurance claim, was an attempt to smear the perception of the British army by outsiders. Perhaps Duquesne thought he could double bluff the rest of the world. A perceived dead man making an insurance claim reeked of high profile news, and public perception would eventually turn to Fritz's enemies as the culprit. He may have thought that, by acting so outlandishly, blame would be placed on those who hated Fritz the most.

Unfortunately, we will never know the truth regarding Duquesne's intentions. It was a facet of his life he chose to brush over when speaking in later life, choosing instead to embellish his accomplishments and tales of heroism.

It also helped that the next chapter of Fritz's life was possibly the one he will be forever known for.

Chapter 12: The Fall of Lord Kitchener

In June 1916, the vessel the HMS *Hampshire* was scheduled to carry Lord Kitchener and his forces from Scapa Flow, Scotland, to Petrograd, Russia, (now St Petersburg) over the span of six days. There, Kitchener would meet with Tsar Nicholas II to discuss a possible union between Britain and Russia, as both countries shared a mutual dislike of the German operation.

Meanwhile, Fritz Duquesne's supposed resurrection had conveniently slipped under the radar of many people, the most important of whom were the British forces. To his enemies, he was still a dead man and no longer a threat. Naturally, Duquesne decided to use his deceased status to his advantage.

Days before Lord Kitchener's voyage set sail, he had been assigned a Russian nobleman to accompany him for translation purposes when he arrived in Petrograd. The nobleman's name was Count Boris Zakravesky.

However, before Zakravesky could meet up with Kitchener in England, German forces received word that a Russian nobleman was making the trip overseas to aid the British. The German army quickly intervened, seizing Zakravesky as he sailed the Baltic coast on an unmarked boat.

Four days later, on June 4th, Kitchener and his men waited at Kings Cross Station in London for the arrival of their Russian translator, unaware of his current status as a German prisoner of war. But, strangely, a young man claiming to be Count Boris Zakravesky did indeed greet Lord Kitchener the same day. The man, a late-thirties Russian gentleman with a shaved head, an exotic complexion, and a minor limp, told him that he was the person who would be accompanying them on their journey. As proof of his credentials, he even conversed with several of Kitchener's men in basic Russian to show them that he was indeed the man he claimed to be.

Of course, Lord Kitchener was none the wiser. He motioned for Count Boris Zakravesky to step aboard the train headed for Inverness, and he and his men followed suit.

Unbeknownst to the English forces of which he was now a part, Count Boris Zakravesky was actually Fritz Duquesne—albeit with minor adjustments to his character. The idea had manifested when it became apparent that Lord Kitchener remained unaware of the real Zakravesky's imprisonment. Using this information, German forces made the decision to infiltrate the British from within. As always, Fritz was the first to offer his services.

Over the years, he had learnt enough of the Russian language to get him by, and even came dressed in the real Zakravesky's clothes and decorations for further proof of his identity. To distinguish him from the man he actually was, he shaved his head and adopted a strange walking pattern. Dressed in Russian regalia, he looked worlds apart from his real self.

Once in Inverness, they took a torpedo boat and boarded the HMS *Hampshire* at Scapa Flow, Scotland. German forces did not know exactly which ship Kitchener was scheduled to board; therefore, it was Fritz's job to alert them once he found out.

According to Fritz, his original plan was something along the following lines:

Once he discovered the name of Kitchener's ship, he would note it down on a piece of paper, along with the ship's intended course, and drop it in the sea for a submarine to later pick up. To avoid any suspicion, Fritz would write his message in a luminous substance, allowing it to stand out in the midnight waters. Once the submarine had the necessary information, it would be wirelessed to a fleet of U-boats waiting on the British coast. They would then descend upon the ship, allowing Fritz to flee overboard and escape to freedom with them. The U-boats would then attack the ship, destroying everything and everyone on board.

They boarded the HMS *Hampshire* around 7:00 a.m., and at 7:44 a.m., Fritz had already begun the procedure. In addition to his luminous messages, he had also arranged several other signals. He told German forces he would hang a pillowcase or a sheet from one of the ship's portholes, or he would drop a distress flare into the water, which would fire after fifteen minutes. As it was still daytime, and the deck was overrun with British troops, Fritz decided to take the distress flare route.

However, it was incredibly turbulent waters for a June morning. There was a grey sky overhead covered with unbroken clouds, with a constant threat of thunderstorms. As Fritz sat in his small cabin, a violent wave crashed onto the ship's deck. It shook the entire vessel, throwing many people on board against walls and onto the ground. Fearing the worst, Fritz pulled on his lifejacket and headed out onto deck. The heavy waves had taken out all lighting on the ship, leaving nothing but a dreary, murky darkness behind.

There, Fritz saw Lord Kitchener and a handful of troops resting their eyes on the waiting lifeboats on board. If they were to make their escape, what would Fritz do? This was the closest he had come to Kitchener in the flesh, and he may never get such an opportunity again. If he wanted to strike, he had to do it soon.

Right then and there, Fritz made his decision: if Kitchener stepped foot on one of the lifeboats, he would pull out his pistol and shoot him dead himself. He may lose his own life in the process or be imprisoned in a British concentration camp for the rest of his days, but he would have carried out that which he swore he would do the day he saw the ashes of his family's farm.

But that would not be the case. A fleet of U-boats descended on the HMS *Hampshire*, having received Fritz's messages. Suddenly, all attention on board turned to them, and silently, the British realised that they had been betrayed. Their secret voyage had been foiled, and their enemies had now surrounded them.

But by whom? The silent question hung in the air. Only Kitchener's most trusted officers were on board, and no one else other than high ranking officials knew anything of the voyage.

But then, Fritz Duquesne emerged from the rabble and stood around ten yards away from Lord Kitchener himself.

Kitchener said nothing, but at that moment, he knew.

Duquesne wanted to tell him everything: how he planned his infiltration of their voyage, all the havoc he'd wreaked in the past, all his escapes, his kills, and his sabotage. He wanted to tell Kitchener exactly why he had vowed to destroy everything he held dear—because Kitchener had done exactly that to him. He wanted to put his pistol against Kitchener's head and pull the trigger himself.

Kitchener's moment of revelation was a short one, as their altercation was quickly interrupted by a violent wave crashing down on deck. Kitchener staggered backwards, lost his balance, and was pulled overboard with the force of the water. Despite the ensuing chaos that followed, Fritz watched it happen, and for now, that would have to be enough.

Fritz had his own escape to worry about. It seemed that all other British officers on board didn't share Kitchener's realization that Fritz was the man responsible, which allowed him to vanish from sight without anyone pursuing him. However, there was also the matter of attempting to save their own lives, as by now the ocean turbulence had reduced the HMS *Hampshire* to a floating piece of wood waiting to sink. All control of the ship had been lost, and the vessel was gradually sinking into the icy waters beneath.

The officers aboard the U-boats recognised Fritz from his Russian uniform and medallions. Fritz fought his way through the tossing waves and was safely pulled aboard—receiving only a series of bruises on his chest and a broken rib in the chaos. The U-boats turned around and headed back to port, leaving the HMS *Hampshire* and everyone on board to sink to their watery graves. Luck was on their side this day, as nature had done the hard work for them. They didn't need to fire a single round to take out Kitchener; they just needed to rescue their saboteur.

Ten days later, reports of the incident reached the general public. All of them reported that the entire crew had gone down with the ship, aside from one:

> *A private soldier appears to have left the ship on one of the rafts, but it is not known what became of him. Some of the reports had said the man had gone over in a small raft, some that he had been picked up by a small boat nearby – and in that sea! – and one was foggily sure that it looked like a submarine periscope. Clearly all of this was wrong, they decided. If it had been one of the Kitchener party, he would have turned up somewhere. A mere private soldier, on an unidentified raft, washed overboard somehow; so they reported the tangled stories.*

The author of this particular piece, and indeed the private soldier in question, were one and the same.

Chapter 13: Desperation

In the ensuing weeks, Fritz Duquesne was considered a hero within the German military. While he hadn't directly caused the fall of Lord Kitchener and his men, he was one of the few officers willing to put his life on the line for the German cause, despite not being one of their countrymen.

There was a constant worry of being called up to assist the German army on the frontlines, but Fritz reassured himself that as he was now almost forty years of age, he was far past the ideal age of a soldier. By late 1917, he was convinced he wouldn't be recruited, and if his skills were needed at all, he would simply attack from the shadows as he had done so many times before.

But there was another issue plaguing Fritz Duquesne, one unrelated to the ongoing war. Throughout 1917, Fritz had masqueraded as a British ambassador by the name of Captain Claude Staughton. His backstory, he claimed, was that he was a French soldier originally drafted to assist the Boers in the

Anglo-Boer War, but he defected to the British side following revelations regarding his loyalty. Of course, this was simply another ruse to get close to British authorities and learn of their intentions. Meanwhile, it had been a year since the supposedly deceased Fritz Duquesne had made fraudulent claims to the Stuyvesant Insurance Company regarding the burning of the *Tennyson* and the Brooklyn warehouse. Stuyvesant were still pursuing the elusive insurance claimer, who they now believed to be the infamous Boer warrior Fritz Duquesne, but with little luck. In their research, they discovered that the same man had recently completed a trek across South Africa and South America with the recently retired Theodore Roosevelt, and so wrote to him for a possible lead on Fritz's whereabouts.

Roosevelt, however, claimed no such knowledge of a person by that name, despite regular interrogatory letters by the Stuyvesant Insurance Company. Eventually, Stuyvesant presented Roosevelt with hard evidence that the two men had met at least three times in the past. Soon enough, Roosevelt confessed that he was aware of the man in question but denied Fritz's involvement in his presidential affairs.

It would be the actions of a woman by the name of Katherine Ferguson that led to Fritz's fraudulent claims coming back to haunt him. Ferguson, a middle-aged widow from the Manhattan area, met with Duquesne (or Captain Claude Staughton, as he went by at the time) multiple times through 1917 at New York parties. Initially, they bonded over their allegiance to the Allies, with Ferguson regularly questioning Staughton on his heroic war stories.

However, it was not genuine curiosity that motivated Ferguson but manipulation and cunning. Almost immediately, Ferguson suspected that the mysterious Captain Claude Staughton was not who he claimed to be. Far from it. During conversation, Claude Staughton would subtly praise the German army for their military tactics and precision, something that stood out dramatically among the Allies-friendly statements thrown around by other partygoers. There was something not right about Captain Claude Staughton, something deceitful.

On their fourth meeting, at a social gathering in Manhattan, Ferguson took Staughton aside and plied him with enough alcohol to kill a lesser man. To uncover the truth, she would need to start small. First, she questioned Staughton on his position regarding the recent Italy-Austria advancements. In October of that year, the Austro-German attack at Caporetto had wiped out the Italian Second Army and led to a triumphant Austrian victory.

'We will drive them off the face of the earth,' said a stuttering Claude Staughton. Clearly, the line between his true self and his invented persona had blurred.

It was the 'we' that caught Ferguson's attention. It seemed an odd choice of words, particularly as the British and Italian forces weren't closely aligned at the time. Therefore, Ferguson deduced, Captain Claude Staughton must have accidentally declared his allegiance to the Austro-German forces.

She continued to ply him with alcohol, keeping her enraged sentiments under control. She told him that she sympathised with his cause.

'Sympathies are not needed by the enemies of the Allies,' said Staughton.

It was a bizarre statement to make, especially for one who had spent the past six months championing the Allied forces. Slowly, Claude Staughton was being unmasked, perhaps through a stubborn inability to disguise his true agenda in such an intoxicated state.

Ferguson poured Staughton another drink, then outrightly said:

'I truly believe the Germans will win the war.'

She impatiently waited for Staughton's response, fearing that she herself may appear to be the German sympathiser if her suspicions about Staughton were incorrect.

'I have no doubt of it,' Staughton said.

And that moment, Ferguson knew she was speaking to a German sympathiser, perhaps more. She continued to ply him for information, speaking highly of the German forces until their conversation consisted of nothing but admiration for the people both Staughton and Ferguson claimed to despise.

The two parted ways later that night. The next day, Katherine Ferguson reported her suspicions to the local police but found them to be somewhat unhelpful. Instead, she voiced her concerns to the federal authorities who made arrangements to meet up with her. Within two days, a federal agent showed up on her doorstep wielding a brown folder. Once inside her home, the agent pulled out several photographs of wanted suspects, among them a picture of the man claiming to be Captain Claude Staughton.

She identified him immediately, and so began the federal hunt for this mysterious British ambassador.

Not only had federal authorities already become aware of Fritz's current position with the German military, but his fraudulent insurance claims had put him on their radar. He was no longer the Boer hero he was once was. Instead, he was a wanted and known criminal. The agent who approached Katherine Ferguson hadn't been aware that the man she spoke of was Fritz Duquesne, it was simply out of happenstance that he fell into their laps.

Duquesne, it seemed, had made a further mistake during his merry conversations with Katherine Ferguson. For some reason, he had told her the truth about where he lived. He hadn't given an exact address, but it was enough for two federal agents to track him down. It was on December 4, 1917, that Fritz Duquesne's New York home was invaded by authorities, ready and willing to haul him to jail.

Fortunately, Fritz wasn't home at the time, but a thorough search of his apartment cemented their belief that this was the man they were looking for. They discovered a collection of photographs, one of which showed Fritz as a British prisoner of war during his time in Bermuda. Others detailed his accomplishments in the South African outback alongside former President Theodore Roosevelt. They found newspaper clippings reporting every bomb explosion aboard ships since the First World War began, including a great number of articles detailing the sinking of the *Tennyson*. At the time, the *Tennyson* incident was the only one that could be confidently attributed to Fritz and was one of the main reasons he currently resided in New York. Perhaps the two most incriminating items the agents discovered were a *Tennyson* shipping invoice and a letter of commendation to Fritz Duquesne from the Austrian Imperial Vice-Consul in Managua.

Everything added up. They had the proof they needed that not only was Fritz Duquesne an undercover German spy, but he had been involving himself in the affairs of the British military under the assumed identity of Captain Claude Staughton. And most importantly of all, they had discovered where he lived.

A neighbour informed the officers that Fritz was currently in Pittsburgh, Pennsylvania, on the lecture circuit, once again under the guise of Captain Claude Staughton. He would supposedly return on December 7th.

And he did return, only to find two arresting officers waiting on his doorstep. He was presented with his charges, 'unlawfully masquerading in the uniform of one of America's allies', and accepted his arrest without putting up a fight, as he had done so many times in the past. Running would only cement his guilt even further. He didn't know what punishments might await him, whether it be imprisonment, banishment, or even death. Indeed, his crimes aboard the *Tennyson* ship were worthy of such penalties, but he could only pray that the evidence against him wasn't hard enough to secure a serious sentence.

Or, he could just try to escape one more time.

Chapter 14: The Mask of Insanity

The Tombs prison was a solid stone fortress in Lower Manhattan, designed to be completely inescapable. Even Fritz Duquesne felt his heart stop when two officers transported him through the ancient archway leading inside. This wasn't an island prison surrounded by wire fences and overworked guardsmen, nor was it made from penetrable brick and mortar. The Tombs prison was a stronghold of Medieval proportions. Once a person was inside, they never came out.

Fritz was held as a 'secret prisoner' in a lone cell in Tombs while legal proceedings regarding his crimes went on without his presence. Exactly what Fritz should be charged with remained widely debated among government lawyers. Fritz's own lawyer argued that he was a naturalised citizen of a country that had declared its neutrality in the overseas conflicts, that he had planned the crime for which he was charged in Brazil—another neutral country—and that the crime itself had been carried out in international waters without Fritz on board. Therefore, the question arose: where would Fritz carry out his sentence?

Naturally, it was Britain that made the biggest plea for him, but both Fritz and his lawyers knew that if Fritz was handed over to British authorities, he would be given a death sentence—whether officially or unofficially.

But there was something else that Fritz knew. While his knowledge of American law was hazy at best, he knew that there was one way to avoid prosecution: the insanity defence.

He was no stranger to acting. For the majority of his life, he'd pretended to be someone he wasn't. However, all his previous roles had been tangibly linked to the person Fritz truly was: a fighter, a hunter, a conman. But for this part, he would certainly need to dig deep.

It was April 1918, six months after the arrest of Captain Claude Staughton. Since his incarceration, he had been nothing short of a model prisoner: compliant, communicative, and relatively quiet. But overnight, Fritz Duquesne became an erratic, menacing lunatic. Gone was the well-dressed, unobtrusive prisoner, and in his place was a shabby, dead-eyed oddball. At every opportunity, he would shout incoherent ramblings down the prison corridors, garnering all manner of attention from staff and other inmates. He grew out his hair and beard and kept them both in a constant state of dishevelled chaos. Several times, guards attempted to usher him from his cell for meals or cleaning, and Fritz would refuse to move unless he could do so completely naked.

On May 2, 1918, a jury was assembled to assess Fritz's mental condition. Their brief was to report whether he was in a 'state of idiocy, imbecility, lunacy or insanity so as to be incapable of understanding the proceeding or making a defence on the trial of said indictment now pending against him, and also as to his sanity at the time of the commission of the alleged crime.'

Fritz's plan was working, but he would need to best a series of professionals to see the fruits of his labour. He knew he had to put on the best performance of his life. This wasn't a mere soldier or British informant he was manipulating; it was a panel of mental health professionals trained to spot genuine signs of insanity.

That's why on the afternoon of May 2nd, Fritz launched himself into the room that he was scheduled to spend three days inside. Dressed in what looked like rags and with greasy hair covering most of his face, the immediate signs of lunacy were obvious. Fritz then screamed: 'Bring up the guns! Bring up the guns! I want you men to watch the enemy. There, there, don't let them close in on you!'

Prison guards interjected, but Fritz wasn't through. He pulled himself towards one of the three psychologists sitting before him and pulled his face directly into his.

'I'll go right there behind the cannon,' he shouted. 'The guns, damn you! Bring up the big ones. I know you want me, need me. I'll be there when you want me, and I'll have the guns. I pledge my soul on it! We have terrible odds to fight against tonight!'

It was total nonsense, but it implied that Fritz was haunted by the horrors of war. He complied with their questioning for the first two days, but on the third, he refused to leave his cell under any circumstances. Additionally, in stark contrast to his previous displays of outlandish gibberish, Fritz refused to speak a single word to his interviewers. Three days later, the commission returned with their verdict. Fritz Joubert Duquesne was insane. They believed that he had been sane at the time he committed the sinking of the *Tennyson* ship, but was now mentally incompetent and therefore unfit to stand trial.

There were doubters, of course, with the City Prison doctor claiming: 'The inmate has developed prison psychosis some time previous to being sent to Bellevue Hospital for observation, that at the present time he has not fully recovered, but that a good portion of his conduct is put on.'

Regardless, the legal standpoint was that Fritz Duquesne was mentally ill, meaning he had escaped the clutches of the British execution squad one more time.

Matteawan State Hospital for the Insane would be his next destination, located eighty miles outside of New York City. To Fritz, the idea of escaping a mental home seemed much easier than escaping an ancient fortress, so once again, he believed that luck was on his side. But what he hadn't anticipated were the horrors he would need to endure while he planned such an escape.

The inmates at Matteawan State Hospital were deranged beyond Fritz's comprehension. In his head, he imagined the occasional wide-eyed stares or sporadic nonsensical on the part of his fellow prisoners, but in reality, it was a constant barrage of madness twenty-four hours a day. One inmate who regularly approached Fritz claimed that the spirit of Napoleon lived inside him, another declared himself to be a steam train and would charge down passageways screeching and whistling. Their real insanity took its toll on Fritz's fake insanity, even causing him to look tame in comparison. He lasted only two months before deciding that he couldn't endure a lengthy sentence in the company of such madness, and so reverted back to the suave, well-spoken man he used to be. He needed patience and peace of mind to hatch an escape plan, and he would find neither at Matteawan State.

Naturally, his zig-zagging caused a little confusion, but Fritz was unconcerned. He was already cooking up another scheme. He pleaded guilty to the fraudulence charges and requested a reevaluation of his mental health, to which the commission found him legally sane and perfectly fit to stand trial. On October 11, 1918, Fritz was hauled back to the Tombs in Manhattan.

Fritz's short stay in Matteawan State had not been without its advantages. Whilst there, Fritz had witnessed a paraplegic gentleman receive round-the-clock care at his bedside, never once seeing him leave his room. According to an orderly, the man was actually a violent criminal but had suffered an accident behind prison bars that rendered him unable to operate his lower body. The man was serving a thirty-year prison sentence but did so in a mental hospital due to his condition.

Fritz saw the man's circumstances, and to his criminal mind, it seemed like the perfect solution.

On October 21st, Fritz stood before Judge Joseph F Mulqueen in General Sessions Court, charged with violating Section 1202 of the penal code: bilking an insurance company. There was no doubt he would be found guilty and handed over to the British forces. While Britain may not have jurisdiction over the punishment for his fraudulent activities, his criminal history would also be considered when deciding the verdict.

Sabotage greatly outweighed fraudulence, and he would be penalised as such.

But the moment Judge Mulqueen prepared to dish out the verdict, Fritz put the first step of his next masterplan into action.

He collapsed to the ground.

The courtroom emptied as a medic was summoned inside. Fritz lay motionless on the ground the whole time, loudly declaring that the bottom half of his body had simply failed him.

It was an odd route to take, even for Fritz Duquesne. Insanity was a different matter— people could, and often did, feign madness to escape conviction. But paralysis was something that could easily be medically determined. If Fritz was to continue this ruse in the long term, he would need to go beyond an Oscar-worthy performance to something else entirely.

The medic ordered Fritz to be returned to his jail cell until he could be taken to the nearby Bellevue Hospital for further examination. Naturally, almost everyone besides the medic in question were convinced that Fritz was simply acting. He had already faked lunacy; what else did he have up his sleeve?

However, the medic addressed the attendees as they huddled outside the courtroom doors.

'There is no doubt that he is paralyzed,' he said.

How exactly Fritz became 'paralyzed' was never investigated by doctors, but they certainly went to extreme lengths to find out if Fritz was lying or not.

It seemed that all official codes of conduct went out the window. A series of trained medical professions administered incredible, almost cruel punishments to Fritz's lower body to uncover the truth. Needles were inserted into his joints, into his muscles, and beneath his toenails. He was hit with blunt objects, sharp objects—anything doctors could find. In a particularly savage act, doctors arranged for a member of the hospital staff to run into the room screaming that a raging fire had just been started on the floor below and that they needed to evacuate immediately to save themselves. The doctors vanished from sight, leaving Fritz alone in his hospital bed.

It was a ruse, of course, and one Fritz played along with. No punishment could make his muscles flinch or his face twinge. No fake fire scare could make him instinctively jump to his feet. They couldn't break him. As far as three medical professionals could tell, Fritz Duquesne was paralyzed from the waist down.

In reality, every needle insertion had caused severe agony, but through some seemingly supernatural willpower, Duquesne had maintained the illusion he was completely unaffected. He later claimed to his lawyer that he possessed the bizarre ability to control his bodily responses to pain, but how true this is remains a mystery.

Fritz was then carried on a stretcher to prison ward 26 and assigned the last bed in the eighteen-bed ward. Conveniently, he found himself directly next to a window overlooking First Avenue, although with a series of iron bars in the foreground.

With his future uncertain, Fritz Duquesne made plans for his final bid for freedom.

Chapter 15: The Last Escape

How exactly Fritz acquired the two hacksaws that eventually helped him secure his freedom is just another mystery in Duquesne lore, but researchers agree that there are two viable possibilities.

The first and most plausible is that one of Fritz's visitors snuck the blades inside during a prearranged meeting. As Fritz was entirely bedridden throughout his six-month stay at Bellevue Hospital, he was often left alone with visitors at his bedside. It would not have been difficult for someone to sneak in two small sawing implements.

Alternatively, a more unlikely theory states that another inmate in the hospital passed the saw blades to Duquesne days before the end of his own sentence. The unnamed prisoner had allegedly planned to use them to tunnel through the walls himself, but couldn't find the willpower to do so, choosing instead to serve his time.

Duquesne, on the other hand, had nothing but willpower. Now considered to be a slightly erratic paralytic by hospital staff, he continued his ruse day and night without ever once stepping out of character. Every day he asked hospital staff to place him in a wheelchair and sit him directly beside the window so that he could observe the outside world. Throughout his entire stay, he never moved his lower body once whilst in the company of others. Only when he was granted private bathroom privileges did he massage his legs and feet to prevent muscle atrophy from setting in.

Each night, Fritz would cover himself in his blanket from head to toe, an act which at first aroused curiosity in hospital staff, but soon became just another odd quirk of the prisoner in ward 26. He told the nurses that it was a primal instinct in hardened war soldiers as it was a method of keeping away rats and insects during the night. However, it was actually all part of his escape plan.

Slowly and silently, Fritz began sawing away at the three iron bars separating him from the window. It quickly became a race against the clock, as on May 19, 1919, Fritz's extradition to Britain was confirmed by the U.S. commissioner Hitchcock. As soon as the legal paperwork had been processed, Fritz would be handed over to the British authorities.

However, only five days after receiving the news, he finally caused enough damage to the cell bars to allow him to pry them open. At midnight that same evening, Fritz squeezed himself through the tiny gap and out of the hospital window.

It was a risky move, and one which needed to be perfectly timed. A police officer patrolled the hospital corridors continuously and personally checked every ward at thirty minute intervals. The moment that the officer's flashlight turned to the next ward on the block, Fritz pulled himself up from his bed and made his last bid for freedom. The sudden shock of having to use his legs caused him pure agony. It had been six long months of bedrest and wheelchair usage, and the daily leg massages had done little to restore all strength to his lower half.

He stuffed his pillow beneath his bedsheets to give the illusion of him sleeping. He silently crept towards the window and thrust himself legs first through the fourteen-inch gap he had spent five months creating. During his incarceration, he had lost considerable weight, something that significantly aided the escape process.

Ward 26 was located on the second floor, meaning there was around a fifteen-foot drop between Fritz and the grassy surface below. There was still the matter of the spiked perimeter to overcome, but it was nothing an experienced adventurer couldn't conquer.

His weakened legs made an arduous task even more difficult. The fall from the second storey window left him momentarily disorientated as intense surges of pain ran up and down his lower body. It took around a minute before his muscles jumped back into action, and so Fritz hurried his way to the first of two perimeters.

His first obstacle was a six foot brick wall, something he could have scaled with ease if not for the lack of sensation in his legs. After multiple attempts, Fritz finally latched onto the top of the wall and pulled himself over. He lowered himself down the other side and prepared for the final hurdle on his path to freedom: a seven-foot iron fence with spiked railings at its peak.

He gripped the vertical bars with his hands and feet and pulled himself up as though climbing a tree. He carefully navigated the spikes, pricking his hands and forearm on several occasions in the process. Finally, he lifted his leg over to the other side of the railings and pushed himself onto First Avenue.

He landed on the pavement with a resounding thud. Once more, his legs felt like they had shattered to dust, but through some ungodly willpower, Fritz picked himself up and sped off into the Manhattan streets. Freedom was his.

Chapter 16: Hiding In Plain Sight

Following Fritz's re-emergence, two major aspects of his life would soon cease to be. Firstly, his marriage to Alice. While he had been imprisoned in the Tombs, Matteawan State, and Bellevue Hospital, Alice decided that she could no longer handle Fritz's lifestyle of treachery and manipulation. According to her, it was 'obvious he had gone German', suggesting she had since become fully aware of his double life. Fritz later claimed that the last he ever saw of her was through the prison bars of his cell in the Tombs, when he 'shook her hand and never saw her again. She filed for divorce in 1919.

Additionally, the war was over. Woodrow Wilson's Presidential reign was transitioning to Warren G. Harding's time in office, and the world looked forward to a peaceful coexistence.

Where would a professional spy fit in?

Unfortunately—and Fritz was the first to realise this—he wouldn't fit in at all. If he wanted to survive, he needed to reinvent himself. He couldn't bring any attention to his real identity or he would be arrested and extradited to England. While the war may have been over, his crimes certainly hadn't been forgotten.

There is little information regarding Duquesne's activities for the next thirteen years; something which is very revealing in itself. If Fritz had indeed continued his life of plundering and sabotaging, he would no doubt be the first person to admit so. The fact he remained so quiet is out of character for the grandiose Fritz, suggesting he genuinely settled to a much quieter life.

Around this time, Fritz became Frank de Trafford Craven. He set up an advertising business in New York and then later moved to the Quigley Production Company, where he worked as an advertising writer and a critic of vaudeville shows for the company's magazines. Fritz returned full swing to the classy, elegant gentleman he often posed as. He built up a great rapport with his colleagues and was generally admired amongst his peers. He continued living in Manhattan under his new pseudonym and, for the second time in his life, amassed a decent amount of wealth and a lifestyle most people would be envious of.

But he was still a wanted man. He never forgot that at any moment, federal officers could storm his home or office with due cause and arrest him and imprison him for life. As the years went by, the possibility seemed less and less likely, but there was a niggling thought that someone may know him for who he truly was.

And on May 23, 1932, thirteen years after his escape from Bellevue Hospital, Detective Thomas Ford marched into the Quigley Production Company offices and put his hand on the shoulder of the man calling himself Frank de Trafford Craven.

'Fritz, you're out of luck at last.'

Duquesne turned around and stared at the detective with a blank expression.

'You are Captain Fritz Duquesne,' continued the detective, 'and a prize picaroon if there was one. You know me, and I know you. You know we've been after you for thirteen years on that British murder charge. You're done. Finished. Washed up.'

But Duquesne protested.

'I am not Duquesne. There has been a complete mistake in identity.'

From out of sight, three more officers approached the scene, all of them with pistols drawn. Fritz yielded, despite his objections, and was hauled out of the building into a waiting police car.

A bizarre spectacle followed. A search through Fritz's possessions uncovered a copy of the book *The Man Who*

Killed Kitchener by Clement Wood, a biography of Fritz's life up until 1919. To many people, it may seem odd for someone to possess a book written about their own life, but to a man of Fritz's ego, it was customary. Rumours that the arrest was a publicity stunt staged by Fritz and Wood were bandied around, but both parties denied any such scheme.

People from Fritz's past were brought into the Manhattan police station to identify if the man in their custody was indeed Duquesne, including Clement Wood.

When Wood stepped in, the first thing he said was: "Hello, Fred Craven."

Duquesne greeted Wood with a nod of his head. Wood then told officers that Craven and Duquesne were not the same person, despite their physical similarities. Wood said he'd last seen Duquesne in 1931 but had also known "Major Craven" for the past five years.

Regardless, that didn't stop the courts sending Fritz to trial. On June 6, 1932, Fritz stood before representatives of the British and United States federal governments charged with murder, conspiracy, and destruction of property.

It became apparent there was a contradiction that worked greatly in Fritz's favour. Although the federal government had spent over a decade hunting Fritz down, the British had recently declared that wartime events were better forgotten. At the request of the Foreign Office, Scotland Yard was reluctant to dig up wartime scandals and renew ill feelings against Britain's former enemies.

So, out of convenience, Fritz Duquesne, aka Frank de Trafford Craven, was declared a free man, but not before another hurdle presented itself. His sabotage aside, there was still the matter of Fritz having escaped a secure hospital-prison unit in 1919, punishable by life imprisonment under Section 1694 of the Penal Code.

Fritz was taken to Yorkville Court and held in the barracks until June 28th. He considered, once more, escaping from the holding cell, but time was not on his side. However, it was in his best interest to stay put, as his verdict shocked almost everyone involved, most of all Fritz.

Judge Greenspan, known for his courtroom drama and theatrics, was the one to decide Fritz's sentence. Everyone expected fireworks, given both Duquesne's and Greenspan's reputation, but it would not be the case. In less than an hour, Greenspan arrived at his verdict:

'The fact that the crime charged—'murder on the high seas'—is not covered by the state laws; that the defendant was held for extradition by federal authorities and that he was delivered for a federal prisoner, lead me to the conclusion that no crime has been committed against the laws of the state of New York, and that the defendant is discharged.'

It was indisputable. Fritz Duquesne was free to live whatever life he wanted. No longer was he a pursued criminal and no longer did he have to hide in the shadows under a fake name. He could be himself without fear of retaliation from his long list of enemies.

But that wouldn't make for a very good story.

Chapter 17: A Hatred Renewed

If not for Fritz's incredible ego, his life story would have certainly been much different.

As a runaway, he seemed content in living out a quiet life involving academic pursuits and steady relationships. But now his true identity had been exposed, such a lifestyle didn't interest him in the slightest. He couldn't be Fritz Duquesne the journalist or Fritz Duquesne the theatre critic; he needed to be Fritz Duquesne the Boer hero. Behind the safety of a pseudonym, he boasted little ego, but as himself, he was driven by it.

It was 1934, and Hitler's Germany were gaining prominence the world over. They were yet to become the universally despised entity they eventually became, but they were steadily taking steps towards it.

Fritz returned to his role as a writer for the Quigley Production Company out of Manhattan, but it was a chance meeting with a gentleman by the name of Colonel Edwin Emerson that launched Fritz back on the espionage path.

Emerson was an elderly American gentleman who'd begun his career as a reporter for a handful of New York newspapers. In many ways, his life shared parallels with Fritz's. They were both war veterans with an embedded hatred of the British, they both had journalistic experience, and both had worked alongside Theodore Roosevelt during his Presidential reign. Emerson travelled the world during the First World War and acted as a war correspondent for the *New York Evening Sun*, although he was captured by the German army and held for several weeks under suspicion of being an American spy.

He wasn't, and he was eventually released. Since then, he joined the Society of American Friends of Germany—a pro-Nazi propaganda organization—and worked his way up to presidential status. In late 1934, Emerson and Duquesne became acquainted. Emerson, it turned out, had connections to the US government. An associate of Emerson's had recently been appointed secretary to direct espionage and propaganda activities, and Fritz's name came up on Emerson's recommendation.

Under the name of John Du Quesne (his given surname at birth), Fritz began a brief career working for US intelligence. Very little is known of what occurred during this time of his life, as extensive effort was made to keep Fritz's name and purpose within the government secret. Between 1934 and 1937, it was his responsibility to closely monitor the German enemies—mostly the British—and report any findings to his superiors. It was the job he was made for, although Fritz felt that deskwork held him back from his true potential, particularly in a role that he was so passionate about.

Fritz held the position until February 4, 1937 when he was terminated for insubordination. Later in life, Fritz would tell a different story, claiming that he voluntarily left the position to pursue field work, but as with most of Fritz's stories, this was simply him rewriting history to fit his ego-driven narrative.

But things would change drastically within the next year. Fritz Duquesne was only a few months away from becoming a crucial cog in the Nazi machine.

Chapter 18: A Hero's End

The outbreak of World War II was on the horizon, and Hitler's Germany were preparing for their descent onto Europe's battlefields. Fritz Duquesne hadn't gone unnoticed by German military officials over the years, given his long and decorated history as an anti-British saboteur. Hitler's intelligence organization, the Abwehr, was delving into the military strategies of its known enemies, in addition to the strategies of the countries it didn't expect to fight against. Its biggest target: the USA.

This is where the infamous Colonel Nikolaus Adolf Fritz Ritter enters the annals of Duquesne lore. Ritter was a Nazi spy later responsible for assembling the largest spy organization ever devised in the United States, and at the centre of the nefarious web: Fritz Joubert Duquesne.

Fritz and Ritter had previously met in 1931 during one of the many pro-Britain affairs Fritz had attended under cover. Ritter, going by a different name at the time (as did

Duquesne), recognised Fritz as one of his own, an intruder in a foreign land working against the Allies from the inside. Although they never spoke on such terms, it was clear they were both aware of the other's deceit. When Duquesne was arrested by the FBI in 1932, this put him on Germany's radar.

Ritter called Fritz and arranged a meeting at his Manhattan apartment on 3rd December 1937. Ritter knew little of Duquesne outside of his heroic tales published in New York papers and magazines, but he understood that Fritz was a fearless adventurer with nerves of steel, and his hatred of the British would drive him into predicaments most people wouldn't dare entertain.

In this apartment, the two spies shared lunch and whisky, and Fritz mesmerised Ritter with his pictures and stories of his recent escapades: manipulating his way out of Tombs prison, breaking free from a secure hospital, and his stint working for US intelligence.

That same afternoon, Ritter made Fritz the offer: gather military intelligence on the United States as part of an international spy ring. He told Fritz he would be working alone, as none of the thirty-three spies would ever come into contact with each other. Ritter handed Fritz a cheque for £100 as a down payment and told him he would receive his first orders shortly, should he agree to the terms.

Fritz agreed. He would be getting paid to do what he loved. Since his legal freedom had been granted four years previously, he had become a nationalised American citizen. His task was to spy on the very country that welcomed him, but ultimately, his personal end game was the total destruction of the British army.

For two years, Fritz would excel in his role as a German spy, even helping to obtain the Norden bombsight and Sperry gyroscope, two of America's most closely-guarded secrets, without America even being aware that Germany had them. In 1939, Ritter sent over William Sebold, the chief contact for his international spy network, to meet and converse with Duquesne on numerous occasions.

But unbeknownst to Fritz and Ritter, it would be the mysterious Sebold who ultimately brought down the Duquesne Spy Ring.

He lived like someone was following him all the time, which he really believed was happening. It is true we were doing just that at the time, but it made no difference, he lived that way anyway.

We thought it would be easy to follow him in the subway; but it was routine for him when travelling by underground train to take an express, change to a local, change back again to an express, and so on. It was a matter of habit for him on going through a revolving door to keep right on going around and out again. He would take an elevator to one floor, then walk down the stairs and out another door. He liked to walk around a corner, stop abruptly, and wait to see if anyone came hurrying around the corner after him. That's why we had trouble finding his home, because we had never followed anyone like him. He was so good it took us four nights to follow him from his so-called office to his apartment, because he was able to lose us the first three nights.

The words of Special Agent Raymond F. Newkirk, the man assigned by William Sebold to watch over Fritz Duquesne at all times.

While the 'Ritter Ring' had gained traction, so had the FBI's knowledge of their existence. William George Sebold was a German-born American ex-soldier whose life shared many parallels with Fritz's. Sebold was forty years old, and was a stocky, heavy gentleman who exuded an aura of natural confidence. As for his heritage and history, Sebold's life story is one of great complexity, and to discuss it in the detail it deserves would require a book of its own. But, like Duquesne, his motivations for dismantling the Ritter Spy Ring can be traced back to a previous incident, this one occurring in 1938.

As Sebold had fought for the German army in the First World War, he had been a target of Ritter prior to the Second World War for his upcoming spy ring. Ritter and Sebold had met, conversed, and arrived at the agreement that he would be the international connection between his spy ring members, but the agreement wasn't without its difficulties. At the time, Sebold and Ritter had met whilst Sebold was visiting his family in Germany. Ritter used this for leverage and explained to Sebold that if he didn't comply with his wishes, his family might suffer an unfortunate accident.

It was a harrowing foreshadowing of the Nazi Germany ideology, and one that William Sebold wasn't at ease with. However, he agreed to Ritter's terms, and together they recruited the thirty-three spies that would become the Duquesne Spy Ring. Sebold was ordered back to America under the assumed identity of 'Harry Sawyer' and tasked with contacting Fritz Duquesne, who would then relay to him the information he had already uncovered.

But prior to leaving Germany, Sebold arranged a meeting with the Consul General in Cologne, Germany, at the US Consulate. There, he informed US officials of what Colonel Ritter had forced him to do. He told them how Ritter had blackmailed him into becoming a spy, but Sebold was adamant he wouldn't betray his country as Ritter had asked. While he was of German descent himself, his loyalty remained to the country that had given him a home. Sebold was referred to the FBI once he reached America, and once there, he was requested to act as a double agent for the federal authorities.

Sebold agreed. He then made contact with Fritz Duquesne, now even more elusive than he once was. Under the instructions of Colonel Ritter, Fritz was told to pass on all intelligence to Sebold, who would then relay it to other German spies, and unbeknownst to everyone else, back to the federal authorities.

The FBI assisted 'Harry Sawyer' in setting up a residence in New York's Times Square. It was a place for members of the spy ring to pass information across to either Sebold or to others in the network using shortwave radio.

This continued for two years. Sebold continued to acquire intelligence from the Duquesne Spy Ring and would pass it on to federal authorities via courier or radio transmittal. The Abwehr was happy with the results, while the FBI's list of Nazi spies continued to grow.

Fritz's own *modus operandi* was to contact aircraft and vehicle companies in the United States that had affiliations with the US and British armies. He would request plans and information—which he said would be used during his academic lectures on military strategy— and relay them to Sebold. The Nazi hideout in Times Square was equipped with hidden cameras and listening devices to capture everything that went on inside, and by June 1941, it seemed that the FBI had all the information they needed. There was a slight concern that perhaps they hadn't infiltrated the Duquesne Spy Ring as quickly as they should. They knew the identities of all of the ring's members, but there were new rings being formed on new radio frequencies that they didn't have access to. This information, coupled with a recent series of bombings on several British vessels, prompted the decision to round up the Duquesne Spy Ring and put them behind bars.

Chapter 19: The Greatest Roundup In US History

Sebold arranged a meeting with Fritz on Wednesday, June 25, 1941 at the Times Square building in New York. Fritz arrived just after 6 a.m. and immediately declared his concern to Sebold.

'It's probably best we do meet where it's well lit,' he said, 'if the room were dark it might make people suspicious about why we're meeting.'

Sebold nodded in agreement, then reassured Fritz that they were in a safe environment. It was likely that Fritz was simply playing the role of a seasoned spy and wasn't acting out of genuine concern. He walked around the room, inspecting every corner for malicious devices. He even approached the two-way mirror, which two FBI agents were standing behind, and glared blankly at his own reflection before combing back his hair.

'Well, it looks like everything is all right,' he said, and so took a seat in front of Sebold.

Their conversation turned to military strategy. Fritz recanted his heroic tales of the Boer war and his sabotage from within the British army, informing Sebold of all the explosive tricks he had learnt over the years. From his sock, he pulled out a white envelope and dropped its contents onto the desk between him and Sebold. Inside were various reports and blueprints for a handful of artillery currently in development. While they talked, Sebold ate a chocolate bar, and Fritz, always eager to show his expertise, was quick to comment.

'If those bars were broken in two, some combustible phosphorous could be placed inside, making it a very small but effective incendiary bomb. Among its disadvantages is its inability to explode in temperatures under 72 degrees. A better bomb can be made of Chiclets, which I've used in the past. Chew the gum thoroughly, then fold it around a phosphorous compound. You can plant them on docks by carrying them in a pocket with a hole in it and letting them fall down the inside of your trouser leg onto the pier while talking to your boss. Then, in a few hours or a day or two, a fire starts, and nobody knows who did it.'

Their meeting concluded at 8:30 a.m. Fritz made an off-hand comment that he could plant a bomb at Hyde Park to take out Roosevelt while he was visiting family in London. Sebold didn't give him a response; all he knew was that they needed to intervene quickly. Duquesne seemingly wasn't content with being a spy. He wanted to continue his life as a saboteur.

Four days later, plans were put into action. It was the evening of Sunday, 29th June, and FBI Assistant Director Earl Connelley addressed a room of special agents in the Federal Building at Foley Square. That night, twenty-three of the Duquesne Spy Ring members would be captured by a team of elite agents—nineteen in New York and four in New Jersey.

Four agents were assigned to each spy, calling for a total of 93.

The same person who had been assigned to watch Fritz from the beginning, Raymond Newkirk, travelled alongside three fellow agents to Duquesne's home in Manhattan. At 7:40 p.m., Raymond knocked on Fritz's apartment door on Seventy-Sixth Street. After a thirty-second wait, Fritz answered, a copy of the *New York Times* in his hands.

'You're under arrest, Fritz.'

Finally, the game was over.

And Fritz Joubert Duquesne had lost.

The importance of the arrests was indicated by the fact that since the enactment of the Espionage Act in 1917 there have been only 19 convictions for its violation. I would consider this to be the largest espionage case developed since the enactment of the act. The arrests were made as a result of counterespionage activity by our agents in which we used the "flytrap" method, which made it possible for us to apprehend such a large number at one time.

The words of J. Edgar Hoover, the FBI Director, following the successful arrests of the twenty-three spies.

A look through Fritz's apartment turned up maps, pictures, diagrams, notes, and letters. There was no denying he was a guilty man and given that he was now 63 years old and wanted for federal crimes, adding another escape to his resume was unlikely.

Twenty-three spies arrived at the FBI headquarters on June 29th, and nineteen pleaded guilty. Although some protested innocence, Sebold-or Harry Sawyer, as they all knew him-— had gathered enough evidence to put them all behind bars that same night. The others would come sporadically, being tracked down in Milwaukee, Detroit, and Argentina, with even a few left standing in New York. By July

1st, 1941, all thirty-three members of the Duquesne Spy Ring were in police custody.

It was a major triumph for the German enemies, and a crushing blow to the Nazi regime. It soon came to light that William Sebold, the trusted masterspy of Colonel Ritter, acted as a double agent to dismantle Ritter's web from within. Sebold was given protection by the German forces, as he was obviously a very wanted man.

But what would become of Fritz Duquesne?

After a lengthy trial and various outlandish statements regarding his innocence, he was eventually sentenced to a total of twenty years in prison and a $2000 fine. He tried to place the blame solely on William Sebold, claiming that he had no intentions of his findings being relayed back to the Nazis. However, the hard evidence said otherwise.

At sixty-five years of age, he was sent to Leavenworth Federal Penitentiary in Kansas to begin his sentence. Considered to be 'one of the most dangerous criminals in the United States', Fritz was proud of his notoriety within the prison system, but it came at a cost. Due to his previous convictions and previous escapes, Fritz was denied parole on two occasions, leaving him to serve his sentence in full. It must have left a bitter taste in Fritz's mouth knowing that his co-conspirators were released years before he was thanks to their lack of infamy. Finally, Fritz was forced to pay for his criminal past.

As the dust of World War II settled and the prominence of the Nazis faded, so did that of Fritz Duquesne. For all he had done, all his adventures and all his tall tales, he did not go down in history as the Boer hero and German masterspy as he had anticipated. Quite the opposite. The latter half of World War II created heroes and villains the likes of which the world hasn't seen since: Adolf Hitler, Heinrich Himmler, Joseph Mengele, and Winston Churchill, Oskar Schindler, to name but a few. Fritz Duquesne received no such acclaim and, perhaps due to unfair overshadowing, was banished to all but obscurity.

In his final years of prison, he turned into something of an unremarkable inmate, long gone the suave ladies' man characteristics and the superhuman willpower to escape any predicament he found himself in. He was a broken, defeated man who simply served his time in peace.

It was on Sunday, September 19, 1954, when 77-year-old Fritz Duquesne was released from his prison cell back into the world. He returned to New York at the government's expense, but it was not the New York he knew, nor was it even the world he knew. He had arrived there fifty-two years earlier as an ambitious, wild-eyed adventurer, albeit an escaped convict at the time. Now, he was a paroled convict, ushered into a community he no longer felt a part of, no longer the faceless chameleon able to blend into his surroundings. He struggled to survive, eventually being placed into two nursing homes by authorities. Prison life had reduced him to a quivering wreck. A severe throat infection had rendered his voice a raspy whisper and, in a cruel twist of irony, a stroke had caused permanent paralysis in his lower body. He often employed the use of a wheelchair to propel himself around, or at the very least a walking cane.

Unable to endure life in a nursing home, Fritz left in 1956 and secured himself an apartment at 526 East Eighty-Third Street. Now almost 80 years of age, he decided he would live the rest of his life in as much peace as possible.

But poor health dogged his every step. A painful fall in his home broke his hip, landing him in hospital for several weeks. Although he was on his way to recovery, he suffered a second stroke on May 24, 1956.

And that was the day the story of Fritz Joubert Duquesne came to an end.

Chapter 20: Legacy

It is a difficult task to pinpoint exactly how Fritz Duquesne slots into history's timeline. He was not a hero—far from it. He was not someone to be revered or admired, but there are certain aspects to Fritz that one can't help but respect.

He was a one-man army, hellbent on bringing down the British Empire. He knowingly entered himself into countless life or death situations, and he escaped them all in ways too theatrical to be believed. For all his negatives, his lies, his manipulation, his sabotage, he possessed just as many likeable attributes: his ambition, his wit, his skill. He was equal parts hero and villain—the anti-hero who occupies the grey area between good and bad. Fritz played the system for most of his life and won, a feat few people can claim. There is no doubt that if Fritz could go back and relive his life, he would make a few changes, despite some claims he made while languishing in a Kansas prison.

In the end, Fritz Duquesne lost. Great Britain won, and Duquesne accepted that defeat with resignation.

Although, if Fritz Joubert Duquesne were still around today, he would no doubt tell a different version of the story.

About Ethan Quinn

Ethan Quinn lives in the beautifully rural county of Herefordshire with his wife and child. In his spare time, he enjoys many different activities, such as walking, bouldering, and playing the traditional English sport of cricket.

Ethan has always been fascinated with people and the stories that they can tell. He believes that people are the most creative, unique, and surprising things on this planet, and some are more extraordinary than others. He strives to find out what drives these exceptional human beings to become what they are and do what they do, which is not always for good!

Ethan has a background in writing, and in 2017 he decided to follow his passion to write in the True Crime Espionage area about the incredible humans that become spies.

When writing he always tries to concentrate on the truth, and highlights what makes these people truly remarkable. This is done with complete honesty and attempting to understand their point of view because as mentioned earlier, these unique individuals didn't always stay within the law.

For more information about the author and his latest releases please visit Ethan Quinn's website:

WWW.ETHANQUINNBOOKS.COM

ETHAN QUINN

Free Espionage Audiobook

If you are interested in reading another unbelievable story of espionage, then please follow the link to download a **FREE** copy of Iron Spy.

WWW.ETHANQUINNBOOKS.COM/FREE-AUDIOBOOK

"Another true tale of little known 'derring - do' by Ethan. A very insightful read of the life of an oft flawed character who demonstrated steely heroism during the Second World War - masterful!" **K.E. Fellows**

"The amazing story of Eddie Chapman until now has been a long lost secret within 20th century wartime history. A great piece of writing from Ethan Quinn to bring this important piece of history to life." **J Thomas**

"...Here's another brilliant double agent story that'll have you hooked from beginning to end. A must read!" **H. Davies**

"Another fantastic biography from Ethan Quinn. This real life story of Eddie Chapman will have you gripped and not wanting to put it down. You won't believe this really happened." **G. Probert**

WWW.ETHANQUINNBOOKS.COM/FREE-AUDIOBOOK

Made in the USA
Columbia, SC
21 December 2019